MW01531191

The Lighter Side of Rectal Surgery

Hannah Publishing LLC
301 E. Carmel Dr.
Suite E400
Carmel IN. 46032

edfriel@sbcglobal.net

Ed Friel

Forward:

Like everybody else in the world, I've said from time to time "I oughta write a book about...

I've always liked to write. I used to write Country songs. Started innocently enough when I would play guitar at weekend BYOB parties back in the '70's when I had hair and thought I looked like Elvis or Johnny Cash. I'd do a Johnny Cash song (usually after several Pabst Blue Ribbons). After I'd finish "I Walk the Line", some bleary eyed drunken friend would say "that there didn't sound like old Johnny"...

So, I decided to write my own songs. That way, nobody could say the song didn't sound like Ed Friel! Hell....I wrote it!

The invention of the laptop computer was the catalyst that made it possible for me to write. Now, if I'm stuck on an airplane or bored senseless at some stupid convention, I can fire that thing up and start to write.

I got serious about writing when Houston Simmons had his stroke. Houston was my father-in-law, and more...after the death of my own father, the man who became...Dad. Houston suffered a massive stroke that left him paralyzed but alert. He lived 15 months after that stroke. I visited him each day, and wrote regular "updates" to family and friends about how he was doing. Several recipients of those e-mails told me I should try to write a book.

Our Minister, Dr. Joan Malick, was one of those recipients. A remarkable speaker/Minister/mentor with a unique sense of humor. She is almost single-handedly responsible for me writing the chapters that follow.

Some of you may forever hold a grudge toward Dr. Joan for encouraging me!

Tom Cochrun and Ben Strout also deserve accolades and high marks for patience. Tom has written several successful books. After drafting two chapters, I asked Tom to read them and "be candid...should I quit and do something more productive?" His answer was encouraging enough to keep me going.

Ben, a seasoned TV writer, labored to edit my drafts. A daunting task, for which I am grateful. Ruth Taylor, a West Virginia writer/historian, did the final proof reading. My long time Assistant at work Peggy Casey, helped me with formatting, corrections and, to my relief, actually laughed out loud at some of my mis-adventures.

My pal John Peaper helped with the cover design and friend Bill Detro put the manuscript into a format the printers could work with. Original cover artwork by Indianapolis artist Kathleen O'Neil Stevens.

Daughter Jennifer and son Matthew dutifully read each chapter in draft form, and provided invaluable help. Matt informed me it was Janet Leigh, and not Lee Remick who starred in "Psycho" (chapter 3). And Jennifer came to my rescue by offering to be my Agent, after innumerable rejections by literary agents from New York to San Diego.

Most of all, I owe a huge debt of gratitude to my wife of 40 years, Agnes Hannah, for tolerating all the time I spent writing, and for allowing me to make her the villain in some of the chapters. Every man should have a wife as supportive of his dreams as I do in Hannah....

I know you're bored with all these "thank yous'" (if you're still reading)...but I also want to say thanks to all the friends who have encouraged me to "hang in there." You know who you are.

Most of all, I know who you are, and you can never imagine how much I treasure your support and encouragement. I will never forget you.

Ed Friel
July 29, 2003
Indianapolis, Indiana

Table of Contents

Copyright Ed Friel 2002

Chapter 1

The Lighter Side of Rectal Surgery

It started out as a hard little bump right at the outer edge of my rectum. I found it one morning as I was….well, you know. I felt around it, discovered it was sore if I pressed it, and immediately assumed I had cancer. And, that I would need an operation. Probably a colostomy. And, that I would spend the rest of whatever was left of my life walking around with my poop oozing out into a glorified sandwich bag attached to my side. All of these thoughts rocketed through my mind in the span of thirty seconds.

I immediately put the whole thing out of my mind, or at least tried to. But over the next few days, that little bump seemed to grow; first the size of a BB, then in a few days a pea. The soreness now was real, and constant. I could no longer sit comfortably. I knew I had to see my Doctor.

My doctor was about my age. Dr. John, I called him. And a pretty good ol'boy. You could joke with him. Nevertheless, there is something particularly intimidating about the thought of having one's rectum examined, especially at close range. That morning, I did my best to get the old tailpipe as clean and fresh as soap and a washrag can manage. On the way to the doctor's office, I tried to drive with my cheeks apart to keep it from sweating. Any effort so as to not offend Dr. John, or embarrass me.

My first obstacle, which I hadn't prepared for, was explaining the reason for my visit to the receptionist, in front of a waiting room full of other patients waiting to be seen. "Yes, Mr. Friel, what are your symptoms?" she asked, her voice echoing through the pin-dropping quiet of the waiting room.
I could feel my face redden as I swallowed and whispered, "Uh….got a bump on my rectum…."

"I'm sorry, sir," she said in a voice that seemed to carry throughout the building, "a what on your rectum?"

Without turning, I could feel the smiles on a few of the faces in the waiting room. No sense in false modesty now, so in a slightly louder voice, I told her it was a bump about the size of a pea on my rectum. She asked, "Is it right on your rectum, or on the cheek?"

My God, why doesn't she just have me drop my pants right here in front of these people? But, I held my composure and said, "It's close enough you could walk. You wouldn't need to take a bus!" She just looked at me blankly and motioned me to wait my turn.

Finally, I was summoned into the examination room. After a little small talk, and with his nurse standing nearby, I told Dr. John about my problem. He said, "Well, drop your pants and shorts and climb up on that table. Lay on your side and draw your knees up."

Ahh, man. Here it is, the moment I'd been dreading. But, I unbuckled my belt and got undressed, trying to act nonchalant, as if I got undressed everyday in a room with an attractive young nurse (wonder what nurses talk about at lunch?), while Dr. John pulled on rubber gloves. No fool, that Dr. John. He said, "Now, Ed, I'm going to spread your cheeks and check the area. You just relax."

Is he kidding? Relax? He's gonna stick his finger in my rear end, press on that throbbing hotspot of pain, and he expects me to relax?? Superman would be quivering in that situation. But, I squeezed my eyes tightly shut and waited.

"Good Lord Ed, relax! You got that thing tighter'n Ft. Knox!"

I desperately tried to relax as he put one hand on my hip and then felt his finger start to work. He was gentle, I guess, but when he squeezed the bump slightly I jerked and uttered a guttural sound that even startled me.

8

The probing continued, albeit a little more gently. After what seemed an eternity, he withdrew his finger, straightened up and said, "Well, I'm not sure what that is, but I don't think it's cancer. Let's just keep an eye on it for a while."

Keep an eye on my rectum. Hmmm. Wonder who gets that assignment? What a visual that conjures up.

So, the days passed. It didn't take keeping an eye on my behind to know things were getting worse. The bump, or whatever it was, was growing. It now felt the size of a golf ball, and about as hard. And painful! I had real difficulty driving. And sitting in my office chair was out of the question. During one meeting with an employee, I actually had to lie down on the floor. There was simply no way to make that sound logical to him. He probably thought I'd had a hard night with Mr. Jack Daniels.

I finally called Dr. John again, and told him that the thing on my rear was swelling, and I'd had all the pain I cared to tolerate. So he scheduled me back in that day, and I went through the disrobing. And once again 'assumed the position' on that hard cold table. This time, Dr. John seemed genuinely concerned as he gently felt around the growth. "I don't like the looks of this," he said slowly. "I want you to see a specialist."

I got my clothes on as he went to his office. I waited for him to come back, wondering what curse had befallen me that I needed a specialist. A rectal specialist! Then I got to thinking about why anyone would be inspired to specialize in the rectum. Does a student in medical school wake up one morning, snap his fingers, and exclaim, "The rectum! I'll specialize in the rectum. It's obviously my calling." "Okay, Ed. You're set up with Dr. Spalding. He's a young guy, but one of the best rectal men in this part of the country."

Hmm, do you suppose that's on his resume, or under the accomplishments section of his Country Club application? Would you put that in an obituary, or on a tombstone?

Next stop, Dr. Spalding's office. My stomach, tied in a knot. Fearing the absolute worst. My swollen butt, throbbing with pain. Feeling as if I alone had been singled out to suffer the worst affliction ever to strike a human being. It was the end of the world.

It got worse after Spalding examined me and told me to get dressed and have a seat.

Thanks, I think I'll stand.

"Well, Mr. Friel , what you have is a rectal cyst. In lay terms, a boil. You need surgery as soon as we can arrange it."

Ahhh! That's it! My life is over. A boil? Those things out of the Bible? Didn't sinners get those things? Wait! I remember my grandmother talking about boils, and lancing them. Old people who drank spoiled milk and didn't bath frequently got boils. And now I have one? How'm I gonna tell ANYONE I got a boil on my butt? I'll be a laughingstock. The butt, literally, of any number of jokes.

Dr. Spalding continued to talk as these dark thoughts raced through my mind. "We'll open the area surgically, and drain it."

"Of what," I asked.

He said, "It's full of pus. And, it's hard enough that there's a lot in there. Probably the consistency of gelatin."

That does it; no Jello for dessert, ever again.

"Surgery like this is pretty routine," he said.

Not to me, it ain't.

The good doctor continued, "And the only real risk is if we happen to cut the sphincter muscle."

Okay; now, he has my full, undivided, riveted attention. "What kind of risk is that," I asked weakly.

"That sphincter muscle is one of the strongest in the entire body. If we cut it, it never heals properly. And we don't want you going around with a weakened sphincter."

Doctor, you can go to the bank with that. We're talking about MY sphincter; not some generic sphincter! I have a closet full of light colored trousers with a lot of wear left in them.

In a daze, I agreed on a date a few days out. The surgery would require a hospital stay of probably two nights, then a week or so to heal and get everything working again. Providing, that is, the ol' sphincter is still in one piece.

I can't remember a worse twenty-four hours than the next. Me? Surgery? Double enemas? Pain. Knives slicing through my most private parts. Blood. Pus. Bedpans. I'd forgotten to ask about bedpans. What about work? I can't miss work! And then, a day or so later, it hit me like a Revelation. Hey, wait! I've never been in an operating room. I've never had anesthesia. Never spent a night in a hospital, being soothed by beautiful caring nurses. This could be an experience right out of Marcus Welby, M.D, or Ben Casey. This could be an ADVENTURE!

My whole outlook changed immediately. I actually started looking forward to the trip to the hospital. I made a mental note to savor and remember every detail. The check-in. The prep. The whole thing. The fear vaporized. Anytime I had a twinge of anxiety, I'd quickly remind myself of the upcoming adventure. I actually started to look forward to the surgery. In fact, I got so caught up in the anticipation of the operation that I insisted on driving myself to the hospital, instead of having my wife take me, like some sick person.

Finally, it was time for the process to begin. I had been lifted onto the operating room table by the orderlies, and was lying on my stomach with my bare behind elevated to make it as accessible as possible.

Dr. Spalding said, "First thing we'll do is to shave the area and prepare it for the incision."

I asked him, "Doctor, is it really necessary for me to stay in the room while you do that?"

Bet they loved a comedian.

The anesthesiologist lowered the mask to me and said, "Count backward from 100 when I put the mask on."

I replied, "Doc, you don't have anything in that tank that can get to me."

After the surgery, Doc told me I'd made it to 97 before I passed out. The day after the surgery, Dr. Spalding came into my room and asked me if I had any pain. I told him I did. I don't tolerate discomfort well. He said, "I'm going to put you on morphine."

Lemme tell you…a guy could get used to morphine. As soon he gave me that shot, I felt myself float up off the bed and onto the back of a white dove. We flew out the window of the hospital. We flew west toward the snow-capped Rockies. I could see the streets of Denver vividly below me. The spectacular details of the streets. Stoplights. Buildings. People at work in the windows. The rush of traffic of Littleton, giving way to the lush, green pine forests of Evergreen. We soared higher.

The sky, incredibly blue. The remarkable shade of blue it gets only over mile high Denver. I was absolutely at peace aboard my beautiful white dove. No fear, just serenity, as I surveyed the breathtaking forest below me.

My dove banked and began to descend into the pine forest. But as we got closer to the tops of the trees, I saw they weren't trees at all. We were descending onto a golf green. We passed the tops of the blades of grass and continued to descend toward the ground. The blades of grass soared hundreds of feet above and around us. Far below, on the ground, I could make out a dot of brilliant red. The closer we got, the bigger that dot became until it blossomed into a full feathered plume of dazzling red on the closed and visored helmet of a Knight in Shining Silver Armor aboard a rearing white stallion…

I related this experience to the doctor the next day. He asked me how I remembered it all. I told him I seemed to drift in and out through the afternoon, and made cryptic notes on an old Reader's Digest. And that was just the stuff I remembered. I wish I could recall the entire hallucination.

That night, I felt the pain return slightly. I told the evening nurse I was uncomfortable. She was pretty cute, short blond hair, glasses, and a nice figure.

This hospital stuff ain't half bad. A new adventure after all.

The nurse came in with my shot. And with the great anticipation of another trip, I felt the needle go in. But almost immediately, something felt dreadfully wrong. I felt my stomach tighten. Bile rose in my throat. I broke out in a sweat. And before I could ask for a towel, or for anything, I vomited unceremoniously all over the bed.

Must have made a wonderful impression on that cute nurse. What DO they talk about when they get together?

Later, they concluded I'm allergic to morphine. So much for any thought of joining the drug culture.

Chapter 2

Did I Just Throw Up at the Country Club? My First Encounter with the Silver Blabbermouth

The first time I had a martini, I had five.

It was also my first night out with my new boss, and customers. Big customers, with titles like Chairman, President, Vice President. My first time to dine at the Country Club in the small city that was home base for the Fortune 500 company that had hired me right out of school about six months earlier. My first night to drive the Company Car. And, the only time I ever threw up in public.

Life was full of promise in that small Indiana town in the mid '60's. My wife and small daughter and I had recently moved, at my new employer's expense (!) from a small un air-conditioned apartment near the Ohio State campus to a small, un air-conditioned apartment near my new job as Sales Engineer. I was so proud of that title, I couldn't see straight. We lived in the only apartment complex in that humid and sticky mid-western town. Our neighbors were other new or recent hires, with young families, living paycheck to paycheck. We all had student loans; loans on our new 'pre-owned' cars....and we were scrimping to save money to buy the proper rep ties and button down shirts preferred by the senior executives of the Company.

Talk about hot. Those apartments were thinly insulated. Built in the late '50's on a lot near a foundry, where the sun beat down mercilessly through the day, and the foundry hum combined at night with the hum of mosquitoes and tree frogs. We kept the windows open hoping for the slightest breeze. I still remember the beads of sweat on our two year old daughter as we would get her ready for bed.

Joe lived a few apartments down with his wife. No kids. Joe had an MBA, while most of us just had our BS in Business, or engineering. Word soon got out that Joe, with his MBA, was making more money than the rest of us; a whopping $50 a month more! (the '60's....remember) Where is the justice, I thought, I work every bit as hard as he does. One Saturday, Joe came home with a window air conditioner. The news quickly swept through the complex; Joe is gonna have air conditioning. Several of us came out to help him get the window unit unloaded. Just think; within an hour, Joe will be relaxing in his bedroom in cool, dry, Air Conditioned comfort. The only way I could deliver Air Conditioning to my family was to take them to Kresge's or the movies. I'll admit to feeling sorry for myself as Joe and a friend wrestled the window unit upstairs to the bedroom in their apartment. I stayed outside to watch them install the unit in the upstairs window, fantasizing that it was our bedroom the unit was being installed in. And, at that point they dropped the air conditioner. As they positioned the window unit on the ledge, something happened, because it simply tilted, slipped from their grip, and crashed to the sidewalk twelve feet below. Pieces flew everywhere.

Joe leaned out the window, incredulous; his eyes wide; his body shaking. He looked at his friend in disgust and screamed " whoever wants that damned thing can have it!!!

Some things just seem to work themselves out.

But! Back to the Big Event. My Night Out With the Boss....

Fred was Vice President of Sales; a stern workaholic who seldom smiled; but a consummate marketing executive who had the respect of his customers and of those of us who worked under him. Fred was a clean desk man; never more than one thing on his desk. He explained it this way: "when the mail comes in" (the 60's, remember…no email; mail the old way) " I sort it for the two or three most important memo's or letters; those I answer right away. The rest goes in a drawer. Every few week's, I clean out the drawer. You'd be astounded at how much of that mail isn't important. Nobody ever follows up on it".

I didn't report directly to Fred, so I was surprised one morning when his secretary called me at my steelcase desk in the sales bullpen and said " Mr. L. wants to see you in his office". I hung up the phone and sat back in my Steelcase chair with a knot forming in my stomach. What had I done? Fred would never call for me unless I'd screwed something up. I thought back over the last few days trying to remember what I could have screwed up to the point it would get to Fred. Maybe I'd offended a customer. Maybe some report or forecast was overdue. I racked my brain, and finally decided I'd better not keep him waiting. I got up, walked down the aisle to his office, where Shirley motioned me in with a nod of her head.

As usual, Fred was at work on a single document on his desk. He looked up at me and said " John Keith and his staff are coming into town to meet me for dinner; they arrive around 5:00 tonight out at the Holiday Inn. I'm taking them to the Country Club. I want you to check out the Company Car, and meet me at the Holiday in the bar at 5:30. You'll drive us to the Club, have dinner with us, and then drive us back to the hotel. In the morning, you'll take them to the airport. And, by the way, wear a suit. "

I was nearly speechless. I uttered something about being honored, but Fred had already gone back to his work and waved me out. John Keith? His staff? This was one of the top names in trucking; the head man at the most prestigious truck maker in America, and one of our biggest customers. He was an Icon; if trucking had been rock 'n roll, he would have been Elvis. And I was going to have dinner with him, his staff, a corporate Vice President, at the Country Club! I knew it! The 'big guys' had seen me in action, concluded I was Executive Material, and had selected me to be a key player in this Very Important Meeting. What next? I wondered who had been the youngest Vice President of this outfit, and if it was possible that honor might fall to me. I started to think about which upscale housing development Vice President Friel would be moving to, what with a well deserved raise accompanying my promotion, and how soon to have some of the senior Executives over for cocktails.

I checked with Shirley about where to pick up the Company Car, then went back to my little Steelcase desk, my head swimming with my incredible good fortune.

Around 4:00, I decided it was time to check out the Company Car, and go home to put on my suit. I owned one suit that I'd bought for $19.00 from an outlet near Ohio State for interviewing, and a green wool sport coat that I'd worn that day, in spite of the 90 degree weather. Dress code in those days was shirt and tie, with either a suit or sport coat. My sport coat was wool. I had a suit, the green wool sport coat, and several pairs of J.C Penney slacks. So dressing for work in the mornings didn't take a lot of imagination.

The Company Car was a '65 Mercury; black, with all the amenities, including Air Conditioning. Quite a step up from my '59 Renault Dauphine that was on its third engine. I drove home slowly in the quiet and cool luxury of that splendid machine, hoping my friends would see me, quite obviously "on my way up." As I changed into my suit back at the apartment,, I told my wife about the important meeting I'd be attending that evening with my good friend's Fred , John, and the other V.P.'s; but I didn't want her to think I was too excited about it.

"It's nothing, really; Fred just asked me to help him entertain the Chairman and President of our largest customer", trying to make it sound as though it was just routine for a Young Man on the Way Up like me to rub shoulders with the great and near great.

It would only dawn on me much later that, in fact, my only role was to drive the car for the evening.

I arrived at the Holiday Inn just before 5:30 and found Fred seated at a table in the bar, a glass of clear liquid in front of him. Even in this setting he was every bit the Boss; expensive pin stripe suit, crisp white shirt offset by a striped maroon tie, closely cropped graying hair, and steel rimmed glasses. I was somewhat intimated and it must have showed. "Relax Eddie; they'll be down in a bit. We'll have a drink here, then go out to the Club....the car clean?" I assured him it was and tried to relax as the waitress approached.

"What would you like", she asked. I hesitated, my mind blank. My experience in bars so far had been limited to college hang-outs when I could even afford to buy a beer on my meager budget. Somehow, ordering a Pabst Blue Ribbon in this atmosphere seemed like a certain faux pas. So, I motioned to Fred's glass, and said "I think I'll have one of those".

Fred's eyebrows rose slightly as he said "so you're a Martini drinker, eh?"

Martini....I had no idea what a martini was, but I said "I like a good martini."

I prayed he wouldn't ask me a question about my martini preferences. All I knew about Martini's was what I'd seen in the movies. Cary Grant sipping what looked like water out of an elegantly stemmed glass; or a picture of a Martini in an ad in Playboy. I had no idea what one was even made of. The only hard liquor I'd been around was the bottle of Early Times My Old Man kept under the kitchen sink. The Old Man wasn't much of a drinker; he'd take a single pull straight from the bottle every weekday when he got home from work, then sit down to supper. That bottle would last for weeks.

My Martini arrived. It was just like the ones I'd seen in the movies. The stemmed glass; the cold, clear liquid, and a single olive on a little plastic spear.

If only the Old Man could see me now, I thought. Sitting in the cool air-conditioned comfort of a well appointed bar; semi new suit; with a genuine Corporate Vice President, about to clink glasses with my Boss, all the while awaiting the Chairman and staff of our biggest customer. I raised my glass and took my first ever sip of a martini.

The martini was icy cold, and silky smooth; with a taste that hinted somewhat of pine needles maybe, and lemon. To my surprise, it had a slightly anesthetizing and not unpleasant effect on my tongue and throat as it went down. So, this is a martini, I thought. Not bad; not bad at all. Life was definitely looking good.

Our guests arrived. The Chairman and President; John Keith himself, his Vice Presidents for Sales, Engineering, and other departments. Four of the top executives in our industry. The waitress reappeared as they settled around the table, and took their drink orders; and I ordered my second martini. Straight up; chilled, no ice. I drained the remains of the first martini as the second one arrived. Starting to feel more at ease in the company of these high powered executives, laughing at their jokes and nodding knowingly as they discussed business.

"Let's have one more round of drinks here, then we'll go to the Club for dinner", Fred said , motioning to the waitress. I ordered my third martini. The sun was just starting to set as we walked across the parking lot to the car. It was just a short trip, so Fred suggested we all go in one car. "Eddie will drive us, and you won't have to worry about following us in your car".

I drove the Company Car to the Country Club. The Club itself was on a lake, at the end of a winding and narrow two lane road. I couldn't figure out why I was having trouble keeping the car on the roadway; several times the wheels dropped onto the shoulder, and I noticed, out of the corner of my eye, that some of my passengers were bracing themselves.

But, we made it, and nothing was said about my driving. We walked into the Country Club, and Fred took us into the bar "to enjoy the view of the lake". We sat at a table out on the long porch that ran the length of the clubhouse. The view was nice; a few sailboats on the lake, expensive homes in the distance, a cool breeze off the lake. First time I'd ever been in a Country Club. Boy, if the Old Man could see me now. I ordered my fourth martini.

Fred and the customers were talking now about their golf game and I noticed I was having a little trouble following some of the conversation. My mind wouldn't seem to stay focused. At one point, one of the group asked me a question, and he had to repeat the question to get my attention. I don't remember what he asked me, or how I answered.

"Well, let's have one more and go in for dinner", Fred said. I ordered my fifth martini.

When the drinks came , Fred said "let's take 'em into the dining room so we can order". I picked up my drink and stood up....and the floor seemed to tilt in several directions at once. I shook my head and regained my balance, trying not to let the customers, or Fred notice that I was having a little trouble walking. What the dickens was happening? I let them go ahead and gingerly walked into the dining room, groping for chair backs for support. What in the world could possibly be wrong with me??

We sat at a table near the back of the crowded dining room, Fred and me at opposite ends of the table, with the customers on either side. We placed our orders; salad, steak, baked potato, and I tried to focus on the conversation. Why was I suddenly so sleepy? And why did it feel like the room was moving? Is it hot in here, or is it just me?

The salads came. When the waiter came back to remove the salad plates, he took my plate, held it to the edge of the table and scraped my salad back onto my plate . I hadn't noticed that I had scattered half my salad onto the table and into my lap.

The steaks came, and I discovered I must have been given a rubber knife and fork . The damned things wouldn't work. I couldn't get that steak cut. And now the room had become oppressively hot. The table was starting to spin…but I had to eat; had to keep up with the rest of the group; couldn't let them see that I was having some kind of problem. Oh no….the steak slipped off my plate. Did anyone notice? I didn't look around to see. I picked it up between my fingers and tried to move my plate to cover the stain on the tablecloth.

I clenched my fork in my left hand and went to work on the steak once more, and this time finally managed to cut it approximately in half. I speared the smaller half and tried to fit it in my mouth, but it was too big, so I tried to at least chew off a bite. And that's when I knew I was going to be sick.

I didn't throw up right there at the table, but I knew I had to get away from there. I could feel my stomach begin to recoil as beads of sweat broke out. I stood up, and tried to orient myself toward the door…why did that door have to be so far away? And were all those people really looking at me? The hostess started to say something to me as I approached, but by now the urgency to get to the bathroom was real. I felt my throat begin to constrict as I entered the hallway….where is that bathroom??

And then it happened. I vomited; on the floor, on my shirt, my pants. I think another couple was in the hallway with me, but it didn't matter; my life was over, and I was going to be sick again.

I made it to the bathroom. Had I just thrown up in the Country Club? With my boss and our top customers sitting in the dining room? Will someone have to mop up my vomit? Will they know it was me? What have I done??? Lord, let this be a nightmare....or strike me dead right here and now.

Fortunately, I was alone in the bathroom as I took stock of myself in the mirror. What a sight. Sweating, my face flushed, hair damp, and hanging over my forehead. Vomit on my shirt, tie and jacket. Why can't I just die right here and now? What am I going to do?

I had to get back to the table. Had to make everyone think nothing had happened. I got several paper towels, wet them and began wiping the debris from the martinis, salad and steak from my outfit. Brushed my teeth and tongue with my finger, and straightened myself up as much as I could. I leaned against the sink, took a number of deep breaths, and took stock of myself. Aside from the bloodshot eyes, stains on my shirt, tie and suit jacket, and the sweat glistening on my forehead, I didn't look too bad. I squinted into the mirror and wondered; Will anybody know that I've been sick? Maybe I can recover from this and pull myself out of this mess.

With trembling hands, I smoothed my hair back into place, and turned to walk back to the dining room. Opening the bathroom door, I hoped that somehow, throwing up had been in my imagination, and that I wouldn't encounter a janitor moping up my mess, or an angry dining room manager ready to toss me bodily out of the place. Looking back, I guess I was drunk enough to think I could just resume my place at the table as if nothing had happened. If I'd been a little more sober and able to think, I probably would have left by the back door and taken my chances after sleeping it off.

So, swaying from the effects of the gin, and in a drunken state of denial, I walked down the hallway and into the dining room. So far, so good. Someone must have cleaned up my mess. The hostess was nowhere in sight, so I carefully eased myself back to the table. The plates had all been cleared and Fred and the customers were talking and smoking. No one seemed to pay any attention to me as I carefully sat down, lest I miss the chair and land unceremoniously on the floor. Through glazed eyes, I looked around the table to see if anyone was aware of my condition. They didn't seem to be, and they were in what appeared to be a serious discussion of issues in the trucking business. I tried to follow the conversation; tried to think of a way to appear coherent and involved. I had to establish the fact that I wasn't affected by the drinks, and that my absence from the table had just been a routine trip to the bathroom. I focused as best I could on what John Keith was saying; something about interest rates. I listened as Fred responded .

Blearily, it came to me; I knew what I had to do. I had to get involved in this conversation! Show them I was alert, knowledgeable, and worthy of being in their company. That my place in this esteemed group was no fluke; that Fred's faith in me as an up and coming executive was not misplaced. I knew I had to ask a question to get involved in this thoughtful discussion; a question that would startle the group with my grasp of our industry and business in general. Putting on what I assumed to be a thoughtful expression, I carefully formulated my question.

There! The pause in the conversation I had been waiting for. I put my arms on the table, looked at Fred and began to speak. "Fled, I mean Fled, what do you think of….I mean…I…you know…" What in the world was wrong with my tongue? I couldn't control it. It seemed to just flop around in my mouth. At the sound of my own garbled voice, I lost my train of thought, and stopped trying to talk; tried to pretend I was thinking.

"I know just what you were thinking, Eddie," Fred said. Then he turned to John and began talking. The others looked at their watches or one another as I sat there, dejected, drunk, wondering what else could go wrong.

Finally, it was over. Fred and our guests stood up, and we started for the door. It had begun to rain. I purposely brought up the rear as they walked down the rain dampened walk to the car. Somehow, I had managed to stagger into the flowerbed beside the walk. I could feel the wetness on my ankles as I sank into the mud. When we got to the car, Fred said, "Better let me drive back to the hotel, Eddie."

Miserably, I gave the keys to Fred and climbed into the back seat, certain I would be fired as soon as the guests were out of earshot. I noticed that everyone tried to squeeze into the front seat; no one seemed to want to share the back seat with me. Guess I must smell pretty bad.

I don't remember what happened when we got back to the hotel. In fact, the next thing I remember is pulling up in front of our apartment in the Company Car, and of throwing up one more time in the grass as I staggered to the door of our apartment. The only good thing about my return home was that my wife was asleep, and unaware of my condition.

The next morning, I was supposed to meet Fred at the hotel, and then take the guests back to the airport where they would meet their private plane. I pulled into the parking lot of the hotel, and spotted Fred standing under the hotel awning. This was it. This is where and how my brief career would end; in the early morning dampness of a gray Indiana day, and I had brought it on myself. How could I face my wife? What would my Dad say? How would we pay our bills? What would I do?

I walked up to meet Fred. He looked at me and said "Morning. You know how to get to the airport? To the private hangar?" I nodded and mumbled that I did, waiting for what was certain to come. Maybe he wouldn't fire me here; he'll probably tell me to come back to his office, where he could fire me in his office, and where I'd have to clean out my desk with everyone looking on.

But he turned to look at the door where John and his staff were just emerging. Everyone shook hands all around, the guests thanking Fred (and me) for a fine evening. Fred was invited to come to their headquarters, and he assured them he'd be out soon. We loaded luggage into the Company Car, and with a final round of handshakes, I drove them to the airport. On the way, I pointed out things of local interest, doing my best to make them forget last night, and trying my best to assume the poise of the Young Man On The Way Up…

At the airport, a final round of handshakes with John Keith and his men. I climbed back in the car, and watched their plane while it taxied out, and until it was airborne and out of sight. Now, there was nothing to do but go back to the office and meet my fate.

I arrived at the office after dropping off the Company Car, and walked to my desk. Everything looked normal; no note to See Fred Immediately. No furtive glances thrown my way by the other Sales Engineers. I glanced in the direction of Fred's office. He was at his desk, head down, concentrating on the single document on his desk. Shirley was typing, glancing occasionally at notes on her desk. The rest of the activity in the bullpen was normal; guys on the phone, secretaries typing; just another day. My head ached and my eyes burned from the short restless night, but I sat down to work, hoping for the best.

The years passed. A few years after the Night of the Martini's, the Company had a layoff, due to business conditions. Rumors were rampant that the number of Sales Engineers would be cut back. We were all nervous; on several occasion's, one of the guys would be called into Fred's office for a closed door meeting; shortly, he would come out, ashen faced; clean out his desk, and leave, generally with a few bitter words to the rest of us about "this chickens**t company.

One day, when I returned from lunch, there was a note on my desk to "See Fred".
My heart jumped; my stomach dropped, and I knew this was it. Crap! I was about to be out of a job. I started toward Fred's office, thinking bitterly that this just wasn't fair. I'd worked hard since my near disastrous night at the Country Club. I walked into Fred's office, my face set grimly to hear the bad news. He looked up and said "looks like a new shirt" (I'd worn the new white button down my wife had bought me out of our meager clothing budget).

"Well", I replied " I always heard the condemned man got a clean outfit before he was executed", not caring how bitter I sounded, since I was about to be canned.

Fred laughed; " what the hell are you talking about?" he asked, leaning back in his chair, a smile on his face.

"Well, I just assumed you called me in here to lay me off"…. Fred slapped the desk with his right hand and, with a grin, said "you're not being laid off! I'm promoting you. You're the new Account Manager for WesTrucks. "
WesTrucks? Me? Account Manager?? This was a prize promotion. A major account, and I'd be in charge, reporting directly to Fred. Later, I

learned that the current Account Manager had just been laid off, and I was taking his place.

Several years later, another promotion, this one to the Atlanta Regional office. Traveling the southern states as a Regional Manager. Two years later a promotion to Division Manager, this time in Toronto, where I had responsibility for marketing activities throughout Canada.

By now, it had been over 10 years since the Night of the Martini's. I was in my office one day when the phone rang. It was Fred, still in his position as Corporate V.P., and the Grand Old Man of Marketing for the company.

"Eddie, I've got to visit a few of the Canadian customers next week; can you meet my plane and go with me to those meetings?" I assured him it would be my pleasure, and told him I'd meet his plane; then we'd go to lunch, and continue on to the appointments. After hanging up, I wondered if it would be safe to ask Fred about that night so many years ago. In all the ensuing years, nothing about that night had ever been mentioned, but I had thought about it many times, and wondered why Fred never brought it up.

So the following week, I met Fred at the airport; he still was a commanding figure; trim, close cropped hair, steel rimmed glasses, and the same stern bearing. But he smiled when we shook hands, and we talked about business in Canada on the way to one of my favorite restaurants.

The waiter came, and Fred ordered a martini, straight up. This was probably 1977, and a drink at lunch was SOP in many businesses. Besides, we were in Toronto, a thousand miles from Company headquarters. I joined Fred in ordering a martini; but I was now older and wiser, and knew the wallop they packed. We settled into the business of ordering. After we placed our order, I decided it was time to find out what Fred had thought about my stupidity that night. After all, it had been over ten years, and my track record with the company was reasonably good. I took a deep breath. "Fred, remember the night back in '65 when you asked me to go to dinner with John Keith and his staff? Fred looked me straight in the eye and said "Yes, I remember. Why do you ask?"

What was that look in his eye? Had I made a mistake in bringing this up now?

But it was too late to turn back, so I continued. "Well, Fred, I had never in my life had a martini before that night"

I laid out the whole story not leaving out a single detail. I could see the beginning of a smile as I described my pride in being asked to go to dinner that evening. When I got to the part about almost falling down when we stood up to go into the dining room, Fred grinned broadly, and laughed out loud when I got to the part about actually throwing up.

"You threw up in the Country Club? That's a riot! Hell, Eddie, I must have been too smashed myself to have noticed; and the other guys must not have been any better off, because this is the first time I've ever heard the story!"

And with that, he called our waiter over, and said" a story like that calls for another drink! Waiter, two more martini's....straight up!!"

Chapter 3

If That's Janet Leigh next Door, I'm Outta here....

I'm old enough to have seen Psycho when the original came out. Majestic Theatre. Chillicothe, Ohio; 1960. We went to the Saturday night showing, probably the early evening feature at 7:00. Those small town theatres generally had 2 showings of the feature on Saturday; 7:00 PM and the late show at 9:30. Took my girl who would become my future wife.

Movies were pretty tame in 1960, but Psycho was different. In one of the opening scenes, Janet Leigh (my crush on her lasted for years) was on a bed in a bra and half slip. My attention was riveted immediately. Talk about Focus! Couldn't take my eyes off her, but tried not to appear too interested, lest my date take offense.

Then, Janet in The Shower Scene; do they actually pay the cameraman who gets to work with her? Is she really naked? On the big screen? Can't be…is she? She must be! Look…wasn't that…rats! Why can't you hold the that camera still??

Then, the stabbing sequence. Talk about scary! The screams in the theatre (one of them mine) nearly drowned out the insanely wild music that helps make that scene so terrifying.

The movie features the Bates Motel. A drab little series of rooms with a small office at one end, typical of the Mom and Pop motels that use to line the two lanes on the edge of small, mid-west towns. Ten rooms, second hand furniture, cheap prints on the walls; a Pepsi machine beside the office. Behind the Bates Motel, on a hill, was the creepiest house I've seen, before or since. The ultimate haunted house. You just knew that place was full of evil. It LOOKED evil. Even in the black and white daylight scenes, that place gave me the creeps.

Fast forward six years. I am now married to Agnes, my date for Psycho. Graduation from Ohio State is two years in the past, and I'm working as a Sales Engineer for a Fortune 500 manufacturer in another small midwestern town. Hot and sticky during the summers, and gray and cold in the winter. But, it was a good company; the job was exciting, and the future looked okay..

One of the best things about the job was the opportunity to travel. I was assigned to some of the small accounts the Company dealt with. I was the go-between guy. It was my responsibility to coordinate the orders, pricing, specifications, and the like for our products with my customers in places like Watertown, New York, Kent, Ohio, and Oshkosh, Wisconsin. Not exactly travel hot spots, but what the heck? I got to know the customer's purchasing and material handling managers by phone initially, and most of our business was handled long distance, or by mail. Written mail. This was long before email, the fax machine, voice messaging, paging, etc.

The Vice President of Sales for the Company was a stern workaholic, but a man respected by his people and worshipped by the customers. He was big on relationships, at a time when the current generation of Relationship Consultants were still pooping in their pampers (a new invention in the mid sixties). We were encouraged, no; expected to visit our accounts a couple of times a year to get to know the people we were dealing with.

One of my accounts was in Middleboro, Massachusetts.. I had yet to actually visit any of the accounts I had, but one day the Chief Engineer for the fire truck builder who used our products called and said " son, its been a long time since anybody from your place was out here. Why don't you come out and update us on your product line?"

Now, my travel up to this point had been limited to vacation trips with my folks back to visit relatives in West Virginia. Six and seven hour car trips with the Old Man driving the old maroon Nash Ambassador, Mom in the front seat, and me, my brother, grandmother, and her pet parakeet (Mike) in a cage. The three of us squeezed into the back seat with that stupid parakeet and his cage. I had been on an airplane just once, when my grandmother and I went to visit my Aunt and cousins in Jacksonville. (We left Mike home on that trip, and my Old Man taught Mike some cuss words while Grandma was away. He used to grin wickedly when Mike would get on a talking streak; "gotohellgotohellgotohell", and my grandmother would just purse her lips and shake her head.)

But now I was in the Big Time; a traveling Sales Engineer. Great title. I loved it, but the truth was I'd gotten out of engineering by the skin of my teeth in my sophomore year. I was encouraged to change majors when I came perilously close to failing Advanced Geometry and Analytical Calculus. I gratefully switched to the School of Business.

I told my boss I'd been asked to travel to Middleboro for a product update, and he barely looked up as he signaled his okay. Wow! That was easy! My first trip on the Expense Account! A cash advance; a seat on a 707; nights in a Holiday Inn. My own rental car. Where the heck was Middleboro, anyway?

I checked with the travel department, and they told me I'd have to fly into Boston, with a plane change in New York City. Then, drive to Middleboro. What incredible good fortune! I'd never been to New York, or Boston, and now I was going in style; surely, there is a Benevolent God watching over me. I would leave Sunday afternoon, so as to be in Middleboro first thing Monday morning. As long as I'm out there, why not continue on to Watertown to meet those folks? No sense spending the Company's money and not getting the best bang for the buck, right? So I scheduled myself to go to Watertown the following Tuesday morning from Boston, then back home late Thursday.

My wife didn't share my excitement about my Week On The East Coast. "Great; while you're out all over the country, I'll be here in this apartment with two babies and no air-conditioning." She sure knew how to bring me back to earth. And, no, she didn't think it would be fun for her and the kids to drive me to the airport, 40 miles away, in our un air-conditioned '59 Renault Dauphine to "see me off for New York.

" Doesn't the company let you rent a car to drive to the airport??" She asked; "why would I want to drag 2 kids up there and back in this heat , just to watch you get on some old airplane??"

Rats. How is she going to appreciate how important I am to this company if she doesn't watch me climb the stairs to the door of that 707, fashionably thin briefcase in my hand. All the wives in the movies watch their men climb aboard fast airplanes as they go off to do battle , wringing their hands at the importance of their man's mission. I'm reminded of June Allyson, for example.

So, that Sunday morning, I packed my one good suit and shirts in the imitation leather suitcase I'd gotten for Christmas from the folks, and sat off for the airport in Indianapolis. First business trip! My wallet full of cash advanced by the company to cover my expenses (the only credit card I had was a Texaco card we used for gas when we took trips back to see the folks in Ohio).

I admit to being somewhat giddy; my first all expense paid airplane trip, bound for New York, then on to Boston! I'd wanted to see New York for years; to see the Empire State Building, the Statue of Liberty, Times Square; and now my flight was being called. I entered the Boeing 707, trying to hide my excitement at the newness of it all. I showed my ticket to the stewardess at the top of the rolling staircase , entered the airplane and took one of the plush leather seats. I was just taking my jacket off when the stewardess approached me and said "this is First Class; your ticket is in the coach section, through those curtains".

The guy in the seat next to me looked at me, smiled and shrugged as if to say " hell, hayseed, I remember my first airplane trip."

I got my briefcase and entered the coach section, row after row of seats, and only about a third of those seats were taken. Flying in the mid-sixties was still pretty much an event. The people who traveled by air were business travelers, or the upscale tourists who could afford to fly. People got dressed up when they took a trip on an airline. They were well behaved and generally friendly; after all, we were now in a fairly elite group; about to take off for New York in a Jet airliner, still somewhat of a novelty back in those innocent times.

Ah, for the old days! Nowadays, air travel is a last resort for many; over-crowed planes, narrow seats jammed inhumanly close; rude passengers….and that invention of the Devil himself, carry on luggage-an! Apparently the rules about carry on luggage apply to absolutely no one, based on the number of times my head has been banged by some idiot dragging a duffel bag on board. And you'd better get to your seat early if you plan to use the microscopic area beneath the seat for your own carry on piece. Otherwise, that overweight guy in sandals, wrinkled shorts and muscle shirt has one of his 3 pieces taking up your space. What is it with these people? Don't any of them own a mirror?? How in the world could they let themselves be seen in public dressed like that? People today must go to garage sales for their airline travel clothes. And don't let me get started on cell phones.

But I'm off the subject. I found a window seat, by myself and settled back to enjoy every minute of the flight. The stewardess' probably pegged me as a first timer, as I tried my best to suppress my excitement as the plane taxied toward the runway.

About an hour later, the stewardess had to raise her voice to get me to tear myself away from the window to get my lunch tray. No "one bag of peanuts or two ?" uttered by an overworked and exasperated flight attendant. This was a 5 course meal, served by a courteous, tastefully uniformed Stewardess; and the food as good as anything I'd ever had at Bob Evans.

As the Captain announced our approach into New York, I was disappointed to learn I'd picked the wrong side of the airplane. "Those of you on the left side of the aircraft have a great view of the Statue of Liberty and the Manhattan skyline; that's the Empire State Building about midway up the Island"

Crap! All I can see out my right side window is the ocean far below, and some nondescript industrial area just coming into view.

As we landed, I strained to see anything that resembled the Empire State Building (86 stories, right? You oughta be able to see anything that big. I swallowed my disappointment as I got my briefcase from under the seat. JFK International! People everywhere, everyone seeming to know exactly where they were going. Except for me. I stood in the vast and packed hallway studying the hieroglyphics on my ticket, trying to figure out how in blazes you knew where to go next. People jostled into me, cursing under their breath; something about 'ignorant tourist'. I finally found a bored gate agent, who looked at me like I was a refugee when I asked how to read my ticket, and then how to find my gate. Shaking his head he showed me the information, and pointed me in the right direction. I think I heard him utter the 'tourist' word. Probably not a compliment, I thought to myself.

I started walking through the crowded hallway in the direction I'd been pointed; head up, chest out; a young businessman On The Way Up! Striding purposefully through JFK International in New York City, my fashionably thin briefcase swinging jauntily by my side. All around me, other obviously successful businessmen, heading off to important meetings, the world economy depending on the important decisions we'd be making as we reached our various destinations. I was lost in the reverie of my thoughts when I slammed loudly and unceremoniously into the glass wall beside the wide doorway leading into the next terminal.

WHAM!

Every square inch of my body made contact with that unyielding glass wall; forehead, nose, shoelaces. The impact at full stride caused me to drop my briefcase and reel backward, struggling to retain my balance. What in God's name had happened? I realized that I'd missed the doorway (it was only 12 feet wide), and had walked smack into the glass wall beside the door.

I looked around and, naturally, people were pointing and snickering; my fashionably thin briefcase had flopped opened when it hit the floor. Pencils, file folders, gum and the latest Playboy littered the floor. I thought I heard someone utter "from the sticks…just gotta be from the sticks."

I checked my nose for damage…none; then stooped to pick up my briefcase and papers. I decided I'd better keep my mind focused on finding my gate. But I couldn't help but wonder what brand of window cleaner they use in New York to make that glass so clear.

I had about two hours before my flight to Boston, so I decided to get something to eat. It would be after 8:00 PM when I arrived in Boston, and I would have to get a rental car and find a hotel somewhere between Boston and Middleboro. I spotted a restaurant on the second level of the airport, not far from my gate. I climbed the stairs, was seated by the hostess, and ordered a gin and tonic. One of the guys at work liked gin and tonics, and it was one of the few mixed drinks I could name. I'd had a near disastrous experience with martini's shortly after taking my new job, and had generally stuck with beer on the occasion's when we would drink; the weekly BYOB parties at the homes of the other guys in the sales department.

My drink came. Manohman…if my Old Man could see me now, seated in a fine restaurant in New York, about to sip on my gin and tonic while waiting for the Seafood Special. Then on to Boston, and a series of real Business Meetings in which I'd impress my customers with my broad product knowledge and profound grasp of complex business issues. My Seafood Special arrived, and I enjoyed my first ever supper in New York. Wait a minute; better start referring to it as Dinner. Don't want my new customers to think I'm just off the farm.

My flight arrived in Boston, and that's when things started to unravel. Where the heck is my suitcase? Boston's airport had a new baggage delivery system that discharged bags onto a chute, and then deposited them on a steel merry-go-round. Not the more sedate system in Indianapolis, where porters took the bags off a cart and placed them on a wide shelf, giving you time to find your bag. And which chute was mine? There must be 15 baggage chutes, all surrounded by milling, pushing passengers, anxious to get to get their bags and to their destinations. (Sixties or not, this was the East Coast, and things moved at a more demanding pace here.)

There was nobody to ask for help; just this sea of impatient humanity, and I was at a loss to know how these people knew which carousel would produce their bags. My stomach knotted and I wistfully pictured myself safe at home, in my well worn recliner. Now, here I was, lost in Boston.

I finally noticed, strictly by accident, the flight numbers above the carousels. I consulted my ticket again, finally found the flight number, and made my way to the right carousel. People were 3 deep around the carousel, and I couldn't get close to it. It was now close to 8:30. I still had to get a rental car, a map, and directions to Middleboro. And find a hotel. Why didn't I take an earlier flight? And what if they lost my bag? How will I shave? What about deodorant? My comb is in that suitcase!

Now there were just a few people waiting for their luggage; most of the other travelers had retrieved their bags and gone on. Just as I was about to give up any hope of ever seeing my bag again, there it was…riding around on that stupid carousel. I nearly cried with relief.

Now, for a rental car. The first counter I went to asked me if I had a reservation. A reservation? What's that? I just need a car.

"Sorry, if you don't have a reservation, I can't help you. Next?" I picked up my bag and looked around, feeling suddenly lost and helpless. And it was at that point that I felt the beginnings of some cramping in my stomach. Noticed for the first time an unpleasant taste in my mouth. What the heck was this? A fishy aftertaste; but I put that out of my mind and went to the next, and then the next, rental car counter.

"You're in luck, bub" said the heavyset woman behind the counter. "We got one. Most people get a reservation before they come to Boston. This your first trip?" She pronounced it "treep" What kind of an accent is that? I smiled weakly, and muttered something about overlooking that detail. Did I detect a smirk?

I asked for directions to Middleboro. She produced a map and quickly went through how to exit the airport and find my route south. She talked fast, and with that thick accent, I only got about half of what she said. But she was already through with me, beckoning me out of line so she could help the next person.

I started in the direction she had pointed me to find my car. Wonder if I ought to try to find a bathroom first? My stomach felt, well, uncertain. But I looked at the time and headed for the car. I still had to find a hotel.

I got the car and started out, looking for the exit. Man, this is a big place. Where the heck is the exit ? There! What did she say about the top of the ramp?

"Damn…watch it!" I hollered, as several cars sped around me on the right, one of the drivers shaking his fist as he went past. Now, cars behind me were blowing their horns as I tried to read the signs, which were suddenly everywhere. I sped up…what was that exit I just passed? Good Lord! How many lanes are there on this road? Why isn't there a sign to Middleboro? Why didn't I study that map? It had started to rain, and fog was moving across the highway. There must have been six lanes of traffic; I had no idea which lane I should be in, but whichever lane it was, I was going to have to get up to speed. Cars were blinking their lights and blowing their horn as I tried frantically to spot some sign that would get me out of this madness. I drove on, hopelessly lost, my stomach tightening from anxiety, and from something else. Could it have been the Seafood Special?

I drove for probably 10 miles. Finally, I spotted an exit for Route something "south". I knew Middleboro was south of Boston, and had no idea in which direction I'd been driving, but 'south' was better, I thought, than whatever direction I was currently headed. Oh, man, my stomach.

So I exited and turned south on a two lane highway. Man, almost 10:00 o'clock, lost somewhere in Massachusetts. No idea where, or even if ,

I'd find a motel; trying very hard to ignore the increasing discomfort in my bowels. Please, Lord, please don't let it be diarrhea.

I found an oldies station on the radio. Anything to keep my mind off my lower tract, and kept driving. No other cars on this dark , wet road; the fog limiting visibility to probably 300 feet; tapping my hand on the steering wheel to the Champs "Tequila" on the tinny rental car radio. I continued to drive. Finally, thankfully, a road sign came into view; Reduce Speed Ahead. Ah! Great! Must mean civilization is somewhere up ahead. Was that a neon sign in the distance? Yes! In the fog ahead, a light blue neon sign…as I got closer, I read "Pilgrim Motel", and, praise Jesus, "vacancy".

I pulled in and stopped in front of the office. Got out in the light rain and walked in to the small office. Rats….where is the clerk? The clock on the wall read 11:10. Was he asleep somewhere? But at that moment I heard a door slam back behind the office counter and a young man in his mid 20's came into view; just over six feet tall, black hair…unshaven, and a crooked grin. One eye focused on me, while the other wandered off to the right.

"Can I help you?" he asked, lisping slightly, in a voice that seemed just a little feminine.

"I need a room for the night. Do you have one?" Then thinking to myself, quick, one with a bathroom.

He smiled his crooked smile and said " all our rooms are filled, but we have a little cabin in back that we rent out occasionally; will that do?" he finished with an ominous chuckle.

If he'd offered me a tent next to an outdoor john, it would have been fine. "Yeah, I'll take it". He smiled his twisted smile and turned the registry to me.

I got my bag out of the car and the clerk took it. Chuckling still, he said "the cabin's right down this path." I followed him around the office and down a gravel path through the rain and fog. Up ahead, in the distance, a single dim yellow bulb glowed. The light on the porch of the cabin. I was starting to get a chill, and couldn't wait for this guy to give me the key and let me get to the bathroom. Please, Lord, let this place have a working bathroom.

He unlocked the door and I followed him in.

We were in a tiny combination living room/bedroom. " This is one of the bedrooms," he said, through his lopsided grin (which eye do I look at, I wondered), "and the other bedroom is in here; and there's the bathroom". I looked in the bathroom. It had one of the old fashioned toilets with the overhead tank and a rusty chain. "Does that work?" I asked him.

"Sometimes it takes a while for the tank to fill, " he said (that grin is beginning to worry me); but you probably won't need to use it more than once or twice."

Boy, if he knew how uncomfortable those cramps were becoming, he'd get out of here so I could get some relief.

He turn and started to open a window. "Don't bother opening a window", I said. It's kind'a chilly in here. I feel like I'm coming down with something."

He continued raising the window as he said, almost musically "oh, I have to open the windows. Daddy's been working on the gas heater, but he thinks it still leaks".

Great, I thought. If I don't die of food poisoning, the gas'll get me. What else could possibly go wrong? Finally, he left, after opening all the windows, and closed the door, leaving me alone. First things first. Yup, diarrhea; third degree diarrhea…why won't my stomach stop cramping? Oh, no. I'm gonna vomit…did vomit. Demonstrating to myself that it is possible to having it run out both ends. What had been in that seafood?

Finally, I was able to stagger weakly out of the bathroom. Thank you, Lord, for making that toilet flush. I stripped off my clothes, too tired to hang them up. I pulled down the covers of the bed, laid down, and pulled the covers up to my chin; and closed my eyes. Maybe I'll feel better in the morning.

Something moved near my ankle. I froze…instantly alert. What the? Then I felt something under my back…and legs. I jumped up, threw the covers back, turned on the light. The bed was alive with silverfish! Hundred's of 'em…maybe millions. About an inch long, with what looked like a pincher on their tail and long antennae waving on the front . Eight or ten legs. They were everywhere, scurrying away from the light, their little feelers waving. I checked quickly to see if any were on me, and backed away from the bed. I shook my head; what now? It's midnight, I'm dying with food poisoning; in a cabin in the middle of nowhere with a leaky gas heater, the place alive with vermin, and Norman Bates' cockeyed cousin over in the next building. I resolved that if I lived through the night, I was getting out of the nightmare that Massachusetts was. And to hell with any customer unfortunate enough to have to call this miserable place home. Surely no boss would ever reprimand me for canceling a trip under these circumstances. Robinson Crusoe didn't have it this tough. John Wayne would be brought to his knees by the situation I'm in. Oh no; I gotta go again. I'll never touch seafood as long as I live.

After another bout with that rusty toilet, I checked the couch in the other room…took the cushions off, looked underneath…it seemed okay. I put all my clothes on and sat down, trying to get some sleep.

I dozed fitfully, and as soon as daylight started to show through the open windows, I was up, still feeling queezy. I checked my clothes and suitcase for silverfish. Used the rusty john one more time. Did I feel bad enough to cancel this demented trip and go back home? Would I get fired over flying all this way, just to turn around and go back? Heck no, I decided. Gary Cooper couldn't have come through this experience without bursting into tears.

My mind was made up. I headed straight back towards Boston, and followed the signs to the airport, determined to get home, take a shower, drink a bucket of Kaopectate, and climb into my bug free bed. I'd figure out how to handle my canceled trip with my boss and my customers when my stomach settled down.

I called my wife from the airport, told her I was coming home; food poisoning, and feeling pretty weak. She asked me if I'd like for her to meet my plane in Indianapolis. (Now that's more like it!), but I told her, no; I'd get a rental car; that she had her hands full with the kids. Might as well milk this for all the sympathy I can get.

I arrived home that afternoon to a concerned and caring wife, who insisted I go to bed right away. "You might have picked up a parasite; maybe you should call the doctor". I smiled bravely and told her I'd be fine after some rest. Just the way John Wayne would have handled it.

The next day, Tuesday, I was back at my little Steelcase desk in the sales bullpen. Told the veteran sales department secretary about my trip, looking for another sympathetic response and maybe some support for my decision. She just looked at me and said "but what was so bad about it that you had to come home early?"

Maybe I had over-reacted a tad.
Later that morning, my boss walked up the isle past the row of identical Steelcase desks. He did a double-take when he saw me, and stopped. "I thought you were traveling this week? I signed an advance for you." I quickly told him my story, embellishing the severity of my food poisoning,but he cut me off, put his hands on his hips, and said "son, I served in World War II. Spent six months getting shot at in the Marshall Islands, ravaged with fever and dysentery, and eaten alive by every kind of bug imaginable. Now, you get that trip rescheduled. And soon". He started to walk away, but stopped, turned , and in a voice that carried throughout the sales department said "and you can get Pepto Bismol anywhere, dammit!!"

I sat down, my face burning, and looked over to where our secretary sat. She was shaking her head with a slight smile on her face.

I picked up my phone and dialed the four diget number…"Hello, travel department?"

This time, at least, I'd know which side of the plane to sit on.

Chapter 4

Move Over, Link Wray

Mom, who championed the purchase of my first guitar.

First time I saw Elvis on television, I knew immediately that I had to get a guitar, learn to play it quickly, and get in a rock and roll band. It was, no doubt, my destiny to entertain the fans, who would surely flock to see and hear me. Look at all those girls screaming at Elvis! Hmmm…Elvis. I may want to change my name to something cooler than Ed.

What a life! He's got his own pink Cadillac, while I have to borrow the Old Man's maroon Nash Ambassador if I want to go on a date. And he's making appearances on the Ed Sullivan show! Instantly, in a Walter Mitty fantasy, I was being introduced by Ed himself, striding on-stage while my family and friends watched me admiringly on national TV. I relived that fantasy over and over.

I started dropping hints about getting a guitar, but my Old Man just wrinkled his nose and said, "Get you a guitar? So you can be one of those sissy boys like that Pelvis fellow?"

Rats. Maybe I'd better work on Mom.

Mom was a little more sympathetic. I did have a birthday coming up, my sixteenth. She asked, "How much do guitars cost? Maybe if they aren't too much, we could think about it."

Money. There was that grim reality check again. Mom and Dad had grown up during the Depression, and were pretty much convinced the next Depression was right around the corner. Especially with, "those rich Kennedys in office."

I had no idea how much a guitar cost but, hey, I was making progress here. I could already hear the first sweet chords emanating from my skilled fingers. A few days later, I was doing homework, and thinking from time to time, "bet Elvis never worries about homework."

Mom came into my room. She had the Sears Roebuck catalog opened to the musical instruments section. "Here's a guitar in the catalog. It's not too much. Maybe we could get that for your birthday."

I took the catalog, and looked at the guitars pictured there. Wow!! One was blue and white! Just like the guitars Phil and Don were pictured with on the latest Everly Brothers album! Much later, I learned their guitars were specially made Gretsch acoustics, worth probably one thousand dollars or more. The one pictured in the catalog was a Silvertone… for sixteen dollars.

But I was already in love with my guitar. Heck, I didn't know Gretsch from Gumdrops. Who was worrying about those details? Lets get it ON ORDER!

I said, "Mom, I think that would be a fine guitar to get started on." I didn't want to seem too eager.

She looked at the picture of the guitar I was admiring and said, "No, not *that* one. *This* one."

I looked at the picture of the guitar she was pointing to. It was a plain brown model with a braided string for a strap, and an outline drawing of a cowboy on a horse on the body. Price: ten dollars and fifty cents.

My heart sank. Mom, I thought to myself, we're talking about the world's next major ROCK 'N ROLL STAR! And, think about your future and Dad's when I start raking in the big bucks from my record sales. Dad could retire from the Prison Service and be my manager. Heck, my thirteen-year-old brother John could even be my tour manager. This was no time to worry about a few dollars.

Trying to sound thoughtful and reasonable I said, "Mom, for another five dollars and fifty cents, we can get better quality, a fine musical instrument. And you know how successful musicians always play the best instruments. Heck, that guy on Lawrence Welk has a Stradivarius violin."

Bingo! I could see that I'd accidentally stumbled onto the ultimate trump card. At the mere mention of Lawrence Welk, Mom immediately saw the logic in spending the extra dough. Buy quality. Spend a little more. Get what you pay for.

She ordered the guitar. I wasn't sure she had cleared it with Dad, but I certainly wasn't going to bring it up. Now the burning question was how soon would it be here?

Mom said, "Six to eight weeks." My birthday was about a month away.

Where were they making that guitar…Pluto? By the time it got here I'd be way too old to for rock and roll.

As the days passed, an idea grew- that rock 'n roll was a fad that would pass before I could ever strapped on my blue and white Silvertone. I imagined Elvis was long forgotten. And I was trying to convince America that they still had to hear from me. Where the devil WAS my guitar? Was the order lost? Had my Old Man shortstopped the process?

Finally, there it was. While I was in school, the Sears truck had delivered it to our small home. It was in the living room when I got home in a big cardboard box. My guitar! My Everly Brothers guitar! I struggled to get the carton open so I could try it out. What's this? No strings? What kind of cheap, rotten trick was this? Then, I found a packet of strings buried deeper in the box…

Crap. For sixteen dollars, Sears could have put the blasted strings on.

I opened the string pack. Six strings all right, but how did you put them on? What was the right order? Should the big, thick string go on top, or on the bottom? There were no directions. I silently cursed the charlatans who were selling "quality" musical instruments. Hell, maybe Sears didn't know how to put the strings on either. That's why they came separately.

But I was ready to PLAY GUITAR. My pal Roger on the next street had an uncle who was a guitar player. Roger had volunteered his uncle to give me a couple of lessons as soon as my guitar was in, and time was wastin'!

Time to get that guitar strung up. I looked at the guitar, and then looked at the picture of Don and Phil on the album cover to see how theirs were strung. Hmm....kinda hard to tell from the photo. But common sense told me the little string belonged on top, and the big string on the bottom, with the others in ascending order of size. I strung the guitar, leaving the actual tuning to Roger's uncle.

I called Roger; "Hey, got my guitar. Do you suppose your uncle would have time to teach me a few licks?"

Roger told me he'd be right over, and we'd walk down to where his uncle lived. I carried that guitar slung casually over my shoulder just as I'd seen Elvis and Buddy and Ricky carry theirs, reveling in the knowledge that our neighbors (and their teen-aged daughters) were watching me, and restraining themselves from running out and asking for my autograph. Roger's uncle was waiting for us on the porch. A pipe fitter for the paper mill south of town, he was relaxing on his front porch in jeans, a white tee-shirt with a pack of Luckys rolled in the sleeve, smoking a cigarette. He was tall and lanky; his hair cut in a butch with the sides left long, combed into a perfect ducktail. "I'll have to give this man credit for his help on one of my albums after I get famous," I thought to myself. It would look good to give credit to the 'little people' who had helped me on my way to the top. Mom and Dad would be proud.

Uncle stood up as we walked up the short front walk. "Lemme see that box," he said, his cigarette bobbing in the corner of his mouth as he spoke. " You left handed?" he asked, looking at me, squinting as smoke drifted into his eye… "No….I'm right handed. Why?"

He grinned, a big grin to signal his amusement. " Son," he said, "you got the strings on backward. We're gonna have to restring this bad boy!"

Crap. I could feel my pal Roger smiling and staring at me, just like I was some goofy puppy that had pooped on the carpet. I couldn't look at him. Just stood there feeling stupid as uncle sat back down in his porch swing and started restringing my guitar.

When he finally got the strings on, he lit another cigarette, and began to tune it. "What'd you have to pay for this thing," he asked, one eye shut against the lazy curl of the smoke from his cigarette.

I told him, and he just shook his head with a slight grin.

"All right, that's about as close as I can get it with these strings. Next time you go to town, see if you can get new strings. These ain't very good."

I started to tell him again that I'd spent a whopping sixteen dollars for that guitar, but caught myself. Maybe a good guitar cost up to fifty dollars, and, he undoubtedly had his own. So I just nodded that yes, next time to town, new strings would have my highest priority. Uncle sat up, reached in his pocket and pulled out a pick. I made a mental note to immediately start carrying a pick in my pocket, the trademark of us serious guitar players. He crossed his feet comfortably, and put his left hand high on the guitar neck. His fingers effortlessly formed a chord.

In no time flat, I thought to myself, I'd be doing that.

He started to pick out some notes I recognized… but what was it? It sure wasn't Duane Eddy or Link Wray, my two favorite guitar heroes at that time. He played for about a minute, occasionally uttering "dammit" when he hit the wrong note.

Hey Uncle, I thought to myself; ol' Duane never hit a wrong note. But then, I thought, Uncle would just blame it on my sixteen-dollar guitar.

He finished playing, leaned back in the swing, took the cigarette from his mouth and flicked the ash into the yard. "That was some pretty good playin'," I said. "What was that?" "Golden Wildwood Flower" he said, taking a drag on his cigarette, "written by Mother Maybelle Carter. Watched her play it on the Opry on TV just last Saturday."

Holy God in Heaven, I thought to myself; Mother Maybelle Carter? I wanted to learn some rock guitar RIGHT NOW, and he was playing country and hillbilly? Instead of launching me on the express elevator to rock guitar greatness, he had me stuck in the bluegrass basement with Mother Maybelle. I tried to hide my disappointment and get back on track. "Do you know any Chuck Berry stuff? Maybe Johnny B. Good?"

He looked at me, then at Roger. "Who's Chuck Berry?"

Who is Chuck Berry? Only the hottest rock guitar player in the universe. The man was a musical moron.

I said, "Chuck Berry does Johnny B. Good. It's the number one record in the country. Larry Lujak plays it all the time on WLS." WLS was the 50,000-watt AM blowtorch out of Chicago. All of us listened to Larry

Lujak at night, when the signal came in loud and clear there in Chillicothe, Ohio.

"Never listen to the stuff," he said, propping my guitar against the porch rail. He stood up and pulled another Lucky Strike from the pack in his sleeve. "I'm a country and western man; Lefty Frizzell, Porter Waggoner; Flatt and Scruggs…. now that's God's music." He lit up, blowing smoke out of the corner of his mouth. " This here rock and roll ain't gonna last, boys. Don't waste your time. It was country and western that built this great nation."

Well, it was now absolutely clear that I had hitched my wagon to a dead horse. I looked at my watch. "I gotta get back to my homework. Got a math test tomorrow."

I thanked Uncle profusely for restringing my guitar, and showing me a few licks. I promised to give Lefty Waggoner a listen, and would take his sage advice about country music. Uncle just grinned and shook his head slightly. Rats. I never could tell a convincing lie.

The next day, after school, I drove my '52 Ford downtown to Chillicothe Music. My '52 Ford was the pride of my young life, my new guitar being second. It was black, with full wheel covers, your basic straight 6-cylinder engine, a manual transmission, and shifter on the steering column. Not a muscle car, but much cooler than the Plymouth it replaced. I'd bought that fine car with the insurance settlement I got after I was rear-ended in the lime green '51 Plymouth I'd bought for one hundred and fifty dollars, my life savings at the time.

I parked in front of Chillicothe Music and went inside. I needed a pick and a guitar book. New strings had to wait. I didn't want to waste time stringing that guitar again. I browsed the music books. Learn to Play the

Flute. Learn the Piano in Your Spare Time. There! Mel Bay's Learn to Play the Guitar!! This had to be a stroke of luck; only one copy of it in the store. The best part was two sure fire words on the cover.... Easy, and Fast. This was more like it. A dollar five lighter in the wallet, I couldn't wait to get home.

I went to my room and closed the door. My brother John was watching Howdy Doody on TV in the living room, so I had the privacy a serious musician needed.

I skipped the first couple of pages called, "How To Read Music." That was for sissies. I'd read where Elvis couldn't read music. I found the pictures of the first three chords ol' Mel said I needed. Let's see...the E chord; 1st finger, 3rd string up, first fret. Second finger...and so on. I looked at my fingers on the guitar neck, and double-checked the picture...perfect! I pressed down and strummed the strings, but all I got was a muffled sound from the strings.

Hmmm...this was gonna take some practice.

I looked at the indentations on my fingers from pressing the strings. I remembered what Mel had told me. "In about two weeks you'll build up a callus on your fingertips, so you'll be able to play without discomfort."

Two weeks? Just to build some lousy calluses? This was Fast and Easy?

At the supper table later Mom said, "There's a man on the second floor of my office building who gives music lessons. I asked him if he gave guitar lessons, and he does. Would you like me to sign you up?"

I glanced uneasily at Dad. He just seemed to grit his teeth as he worked at cutting the left over ham we were having. I thought for a second. Somehow,

I couldn't see Elvis taking guitar lessons. But I wasn't making too much headway with Mel. Maybe a few lessons from a real guitar instructor was the answer after all.

"Sure," I said.

Now, it was Dad's turn. He asked Mom, "How much are these lessons anyway?"

"Now, Carl, " she said. "It's only a dollar for 30 minutes."

Dad turned to me. "Now, when I was your age...."

I thought, Oh no, here we go again...

Worked for a quarter an hour. Split wood. Walked to school. Didn't wear shoes in the summer 'cause I had to save 'em for winter.

I knew this wasn't the last time I'd hear "The Lecture."But Mom prevailed and signed me up. A few days later, I made my way downtown with my guitar in the cardboard case. I trooped upstairs to my teacher's studio, over Mom's office at the Insurance Agency, hoping people would notice me carrying my guitar. Carrying that guitar around was most of the fun of owning it so far. At least people might think I could play it.

Good night, I thought, on meeting my teacher for the first time. This guy is older than dirt! Bet he's never heard of Chuck Berry either. Mr. Witherspoon was probably 70. Short, thin with a white fringe of hair around his otherwise bald little head. Rimless glasses on the end of his nose. An old cardigan sweater that he had mis-buttoned. Baggy suit pants and bedroom slippers. I've missed that Express Elevator again, I thought to myself. Another disappointment on the road to rock stardom

I unpacked my guitar while Mr. Witherspoon pulled up the two folding chairs and a music stand an a....what the heck was that? "This is a metronome" he said. "It helps you keep time to the music." It looked like a relic from the Middle Ages.

He took my guitar, and strummed it to check the tuning. "Hmmm, a Silvertone...from Sears Roebuck?" he asked, cocking his head slightly.

Yup! Cost sixteen bucks," I said proudly.

"I assumed as much," he sighed. "We'd best get started. Here's the music for the notes we'll practice on the first string."

Music? I thought. You're gonna teach me music? Elvis never....and just the first string? This is gonna take forever! I agonized through the lesson-plink, plink , plink....over and over. Three stupid notes, and not a one of them sounded like "Rebel Rouser." Duane Eddy would be laughing his butt off if he could see me. Plink, plink, plink. I told Mom later I didn't think I'd be going back. A dollar for 30 minutes did sound a little extravagant to me. Out of the corner of my eye, I could see the slightest hint of a smile on the Old Man's face.

I gave Mel another chance. Every evening I'd practice the chords pictured, and Mel was right. I developed the promised calluses. Finally, I was able to play the E chord without muffling the strings.

Jody Reynolds had a hit record out at about that time, probably 1960 called "Endless Sea," a simple 3- chord song. I thought it sounded like Jody was playing the E chord. Sure enough, he was. And, whaddya know....the other 2 chords were in fact, A and B. Just like in the book. My respect for Mel went up a notch. I bought the record, and sat in front of the hi-fi, playing along with the record. E, then A...then B. Man, I'm on my way!

Even my Old Man was impressed. He walked in one day and said in an astonished tone, "You can actually play that thing!"

Hey Dad, I thought, it's in my blood. It's my destiny.

Lefty Waggoner, eat your heart out. Ed Friel's about to Blast Off!

I got into a band with a friend at school. He told me he played guitar. I said I did too. He knew a guy who had a set of drums, and another kid who wanted to sing. My friend Danny was a sax player in the school band. Every rock band worth it's salt in those days had a sax, so we were set. We agreed to all get together. The drummer, Walt, lived with his Mom just outside of town, and she worked the 3:00-11:00 shift driving a forklift at the mill. So we even had a place to practice, Walt's basement.

Chuck, the guitar player, had a Fender Strat, just like Buddy Holly's. Walt had a basic drum set. Danny had his sax from the school band, and Willie sang in his church. We were gonna be sensational.

My first practice with a real rock band! Talk about exciting! I unpacked by blue and white Silvertone. Chuck came over to examine it; played a couple of chords, and said, "Maybe you ought to get some new strings before our first appearance."

We got tuned up, and stood around the drum set. Chuck knew a song called "Sugaree" a regional hit by a band out of Cincinnati. He played it through. Walt caught on to the beat. Danny chimed in with the sax, and Willy, who knew the song, was wailin'!

As for me, I was completely lost. Chuck was playing lead, and as the rhythm guitar player, I was supposed to follow him. None of the chords I played sounded right. Chuck played on…watching my shaking hands, and stopped.

"I thought you could play that thing," he said.

"Guess I'm a little rusty on that song," I replied. "Rusty? You ain't played the right chord yet!"

My face reddened as the other guys looked at me. Chuck said, "Well , I don't know anybody else who has a guitar. Fellows, take a break while I teach our rhythm guy how to play the song."

I sighed with genuine relief. I thought he was going to fire me on the spot. Give my place in the band to another guitar player. I could have hugged him.

I knew the chords by name by now…just couldn't put 'em together in a song, except for "Endless Sleep." Chuck patiently went through 'Sugaree' with me a few times. Showed me where to change chords, and finally said, "Just keep your eye on me. I'll tell you which chord to play." Pretty nice of Chuck. He was a redhead, and I thought guys with red hair were short tempered and always spoiling for a fight. But Chuck worked with me, thus assuring my place in the band.

At that first rehearsal, we learned three songs; Sugaree, Walk, Don't Run, an instrumental, (Willy just snapped his fingers and boogied during that one) and a really simplified three- chord version of Night Train.

We were ready. We were "The Contours," a name Chuck liked, and since he had a Fender Strat, and an old station wagon to haul our gear, he got to pick. I was officially the Rhythm Guitar Player in a genuine Rock

Band. The Contours! Chillicothe today, American Bandstand tomorrow. Nothing could stop The Contours.

We got our first gig from Chuck's friend in Jackson, about twenty-five miles away. There was a Saturday night sock hop at the local American Legion hall, with a disc jockey spinning records. Chuck allowed as to how The Contours were available to play a set, and that was that...no audition; we were hired. Free. They couldn't afford to pay us.

No problem! This was our big opportunity! People would see us, word would spread. Wasn't this the way Little Richard started out?

So, with one rehearsal under our belts, we set up our instruments under the surprisingly excited gaze of some of the teenage girls in the crowd. They'd probably never seen a real rock band, and here we were right in their midst. We were introduced midway through the sock hop by the local DJ; "Lets hear it for the Contours!" We launched into Sugaree, my hands shaking from excitement as I did my best to watch Chuck and follow the chord changes. When we finished Sugaree, the girls in front of the stage were clapping and screaming, just like they had seen the crowd do on American Bandstand. But, I noticed most of the guys standing towards the back of the hall, just staring at us. Uh oh. We got through Walk, Don't Run and Night Train without too many crippling errors, and set our instruments down. The DJ put on a record, and came over to us. He asked us how long we'd been together. We told him this was our first appearance. "I kinda thought that," he said.

But we'd done it. I had just finished my first appearance with a rock band. My dream was coming true! And, some of the girls actually wanted our autographs! I was signing a scrap of paper for one of the girls when a huge crewcut guy in a Jackson Football jacket tapped me roughly on the chest. He looked down at me and said "You keep messin' with my girl, Blackie and I'm gonna kick your ass 'till my shoes catch on fire".

I glanced down. He was wearing engineer boots, black with a square heel. My rear end would be the anatomical equivalent of Hiroshima before those things even got warm, I thought.

No wonder Elvis had all those bodyguards.

As we worked on our three songs in Walt's basement over the next few weeks, we decided to let Walt have a drum solo in the middle of Night Train. Chuck thought it would be cool if the rest of us set down our instruments and left the stage while Walt pounded away. Then we'd come back on stage, backs to the audience, put our guitars and sax on, and at just the right moment , whirl around and start playing again. It would set the crowd wild, we thought.

We got another gig. This time it was the Union Hall down by the mill for a crowd of about 50 kids, with a few adults as chaperones. "Sugaree" got pretty much the same crowd reaction. A few girls up front screaming. Most of the guys gazing at us sullenly from the back. The adults just stared at us. We followed with "Walk, Don't Run. By now, I could get through this without watching Chuck. Then, for our finale, "Night Train," with a show stopping performance of our drum solo routine.

Danny started blowing the opening notes of Night Train with Chuck and me filling in. Willie was on fire with the vocals, "Niiiiight Traiiiiin…that took my baby far away…"

We took off our instruments. Walt pounded his drum set like he was possessed. Willie, Danny, Chuck and I sauntered importantly to the side of the room, where Chuck lit up. After a few minutes, we looked at each other, smiled and walked back on stage. The crowd had to be loving this, I thought. Backs to the audience, we strapped on our guitars. Danny fastened his sax to the neck strap…and we whirled around.

The neck of my guitar hit Danny's sax just as he brought it to his lips. The mouthpiece was driven sharply into his mouth, splitting his lip...just as Chuck started to play. I dropped my pick. Danny was holding his fingers to his swelling and bleeding lip. I stood there as Danny gave me a dirty look, and walked off the stage to check on the damage to his mouth. Chuck and Walt brought Night Train to a ragged close, and we left the stage.

I went to check on Danny. As I passed the table of adults, one of them said, "Y'all boys may want to work on your choreography else that sax player ain't gonna have any teeth left."

The world needs more comedians, I thought to myself. When I'm on Bandstand, Jack, you're still gonna be takin' up space at this Union Hall workin' for a living at that stupid mill.

Over the next few months, the Contours played their 3- song set at another half dozen sock hops around the area. Still all for free. Then one day Chuck called and said, "We've been hired to play for the Huntington High Prom. We're gonna get twenty-five dollars!"

"Apiece?" I asked, not believing our good fortune.

"Well, no," he said. "We'll have to split it, but hell, man, we're actually getting paid to perform!"

Now, we really should have thought this through a little better. There would be a DJ playing records, but we were expected to do 3 sets with three songs each set. After all, this wasn't a sock hop. This was the Prom.

We all piled into Chuck's Station Wagon on that memorable Friday evening. We were dressed in our Contours uniform- white dress shirt, black pants, white socks and black shoes. Chuck and Walt didn't own a long sleeved white shirt. Theirs were short sleeved. Wille's was white, with a faint brown splotch near the shoulder where the iron had stayed too long. But by golly, we thought we were hot stuff.

This was the biggest crowd we'd ever played for, probably 150 high school teens dressed in their finest, and a group of teachers acting as chaperones. Huntington was a high school out in the country, so there wasn't a tux in sight. Nevertheless, it was a good crowd. The gym was decorated with strands of crepe in the school colors, and colored spotlights added to the atmosphere. The DJ was from the local radio station. He was dressed in a suit. His equipment had the station call letters, WCHI, prominently featured. This was as close to the big time as we had ever been.

The DJ played records for the first half hour, while we set up our gear. We stayed backstage, out of sight of the crowd. After all, we were the Talent. We were above taking part in the action on the dance floor.

The DJ came looking for us behind the stage curtain. "Okay, guys, you ready?" We nodded, ready to knock their socks off. And we did. We had those three songs down pretty well by now. We'd gotten over the stage fright, and we'd rehearsed the routine in Night Train to insure Danny would suffer no further indignities. Willie was in good voice, and Chuck was impressive on lead guitar. We got a strong welcome from the crowd. The girls were screaming…and even the guys seemed not to mind the attention we were getting.

After our first set, the DJ told us, "That was pretty good fellows. You'll be on again in about 30 minutes. What's in your second set?"

And that's when it sunk in. I thought, uh oh, maybe we should have worked a little harder on some of the songs we were trying to learn.

We didn't really answer him. Chuck mumbled something about how much the crowd liked Night Train.

Back at his microphone, the DJ introduced The Belmont's latest hit record.

Backstage, Chuck told us, "Let's mix up the order next time. Walk, Don't Run first, then Night Train, then Sugaree." It was the only thing we could do.

We were introduced again.and, went through our set. The crowd wasn't as receptive this time, I noticed. Not as much screaming, and some of the kids just stared at us. Out of the corner of my eye, I could see the DJ looking at his watch and frowning. When we finished, there was polite clapping from the crowd.

When the DJ came over to us backstage, he was still frowning. "You guys got one more set. You can't go out there and play those same three songs. This is a Prom. This is my reputation! I'm paying you guys. Don't you know anything else?" He started to walk away, but came back. "Surely you guys know something else!" He walked out to his turntables, smiled at the crowd, and introduced Ronnie and the Daytona's latest hit, "Little GTO."

We had been working on "Chain Gang," that great Sam Cooke hit. We hadn't gotten it down. "Chain Gang" had five chords, and some tricky chord changes. We were a three-chord band. Our only salvation was with Willie. He could really sing. "Guys, it's Chain Gang. We gotta do it," Chuck said. "We'll do "Chain Gang" and finish with "Night Train." Willie, give it all you got. You got to get us through this."

I started to panic. What chord did we start in? I couldn't ask Chuck. He was sweating as it was. No sense in ruining his mood further by telling him I didn't remember ANY of the chords. I thought, maybe I could watch him and fake it.

The DJ came back. "All right you guys, what's your first number? And don't tell me Sugaree." Chuck told him to introduce "the Contours' version of Chain Gang."

My heart was pounding, my stomach in a knot.

"Ladies and gentlemen, for their final set, let's hear it for the Contours doing Chain Gang!"

The curtain slid open, and we were on stage. The blinding spotlights were trained on us. My knees began shaking.

Willie started in, strong as usual.

"All day long I hear the sounds of the men, workin' on the chain gang."

Chuck fell in with the C chord. Walt's drums picked up the pace, but with the wrong beat. Way too fast. I strummed the C chord, but Chuck changed. Where did he go? I played an F. Wrong…oh crap! Danny played in the wrong key completely. God help us.

Willie, still doing his best, looked around and caught my eye.

I thought, God, look at that expression on his face. We're killing him.

Chuck turned up his guitar volume, trying to drown me out. At that moment, the spotlights blinked off. Chuck was still playing, but the power to our amp was cut off. Danny's sax, was the last sound I heard from us.

Bobby Rydell's music suddenly filled the gym. The DJ had killed our power, turned off our mikes, and put on a record.

I looked out at the crowd. They were just staring at us. No applause, no screaming. They just stared, then slowly resumed dancing or talking among themselves.

The DJ confronted us. "That's it! Pack up. You're through. And forget the dough. You just better hope this doesn't reflect on me. Now...OUT!" All we could do was pack up...silently. I put my guitar in the cardboard case. I helped Walt carry his stuff to the station wagon. The rest of the guys followed. No one stopped us for an autograph.

We drove back to Walt's place in silence. We were devastated. We had embarrassed ourselves in front of 150 kids. Word would spread, and we'd be a joke for weeks to come.

I didn't see Willie after that. A year or so later, I ran into Chuck at the paper mill. I had a summer job there, saving my money for my sophomore year at Ohio U. Chuck was working at the mill full time as 'third hand' on one of the paper machines. We didn't spend much time reminiscing. We just greeted one another and, parted with a promise to get together sometime...knowing we never would.

It was the end of the Contours, and the end of my boyhood dream of Rock Stardom.

Chapter 5

DJ Daze

DJ Daze, WCHI, Chillicothe, Ohio 1960

I got a job on the radio. Sixteen years old. Not exactly "A Star is Born," but a big deal to me.

Ever since I could remember, I'd been fascinated by radio; by the voices coming out of that magic box! Who were those people…what did they look like?. What a great job! Working in a modern studio, behind a microphone, talking to millions of people, and getting paid for it. Why would anyone want to do anything else? You actually get paid? For real? Heck, if I could get a job on radio, I'd do it for free.

Living on top of a remote mountain in West Virginia, and listening to radio stations from Pittsburg, Wheeling….Cincinnati… was magic! Those voices meant there was another world out there; where people lived in modern cities; went to work in suits and ties….and got paid to be entertaining! I tried to picture the people behind those voices. I envied them. I fantasized I'd be on the radio when I grew up.

I was probably 12 years old when I made a microphone out of a chunk of an old 2 x 4. I found a picture of an announcer talking into a mike. I carved that chunk of lumber to look like the microphone in the picture, then used a pencil to make the little holes. It looked pretty good. While my brother John was watching cartoons, and I had our room to myself, I'd shut the bedroom door, put that microphone on my desk, and pretend to be broadcasting to the world.

We had moved to Chillicothe by this time, and Chillicothe had two AM radio stations. Any time I'd go out in the car with Mom or Dad, I'd silently hope they'd drive by one of the radio stations. It was cool driving by when we were listening to the station. Boy, if I could just go in to look around.…There was a newsman on WCHI with the deepest voice I'd ever heard. The guy had to be in his 50's, I thought; and weigh about 300 pounds. You know how you form a mental picture of someone just listening to their voice? Well, that's how I pictured Steve Stevens. An old, polished, professional, real live Radio Announcer.

One day, when I was just starting my senior year at Chillicothe High, we had to go to assembly for an orientation program. The Principal, Mr. Wiley, was speaking. I was whispering to my pal Roger….not really paying attention to what Mr. W was saying. But then I heard him say something about Steve Stevens….I was instantly alert: Steve Stevens? Here? To speak to us? I was actually going to see a real Radio Announcer…in person.

But where was he? Nobody on the stage except for Mr. W at the podium…Ah! Behind the curtain! That's where he is….gotta be.

Mr. Wiley was saying " and now, let's welcome Steve Stevens of WCHI to our microphone "

I stared at the curtains, but no one came out. But then, the kids in the front of the auditorium started applauding. I looked over to where they were motioning and saw a kid walking up to the stage. I'd seen that kid in the hallways during class changes, but didn't know him. Where the heck is that idiot going, I thought to myself.

The student walked to the podium, shook hands with Mr. Wiley; then moved to the mike and began speaking, in that wonderously deep resonate voice " Good morning , fellow Cavalier fans (the football team was called the Cavaliers). I'm Steve Stevens".

I almost fell out of my seat. THAT'S Steve Stevens? That little runt? Can't be….can it? It was. Steve Stevens was a senior, just like me. Same height, maybe a tad heavier, with a crewcut. Nowhere near 50, or 300 pounds.

I didn't hear anything Steve said. A jumble of thoughts ricocheted through my mind; 'he's my age…how the devil did he get on the radio? What's he make? Probably $35,000 dollars….(he's in the entertainment business, right? Those guys make serious bucks)! How DID he get on radio?? I'm the one that wants to be on radio!'

I resolved to get to know Steve Stevens. No, not just get to know him;.he'd be my best friend. Once we got to know one another, I'd casually drop a hint about maybe trying out for a job as an announcer.

My chance came within a week. I was in the school john, relieving myself, and someone walked up to the next urinal. I glanced over, (keeping my eyes at eye level)…and nearly lost control of my aim. Steve Stevens! I'm peeing right next to Steve Stevens of WCHI Radio….my big chance! What to say? Don't miss this chance; they say the Lord works in mysterious ways. Maybe HE was responsible for co-ordinating the timing of our bladders.

We finished and were both washing our hands…

"You do a really radio job on the great, Steve" ….ah, crap…how did that happen? Did I just say what I think I said??

"I mean, I really enjoy listening to you do the news". Wonderful. Now I feel my face turning red.

"Thank you" he replied in his Steve Stevens voice, and started to walk out of the bathroom. He's walking out; my big chance, and he's leaving!! I gotta say something.

"Say Steve, how does someone get a chance to work in radio?"…. ratsratsrats….what a stupid thing to say. Bet he hears that all the time. I was mentally kicking myself for being so stupid.

But, instead of walking out the door, he stopped, turned to me and said, "well, the best thing is to come down to the station, make an audition tape, and get the Chief Announcer to listen to it."

I couldn't believe my ears. STEVE STEVENS himself had just spoken to me. Actually given me some advice! Wait; maybe this is some cruel trick. Maybe he's just making fun of me.

" You mean, just come to the station and make a tape? Who would I talk to there?'

" Are you really serious about getting into radio?" he came back into the bathroom. "It's a serious time commitment. Lot's of weekend work. Early mornings too. And it's not as glamorous as you might think"

Steverino, ol' buddy ol pal, (I thought to myself) if you want to experience a non-glamorous job, come with me on my paper route some evening.

I looked Steve directly in the eye and said "Steve, I'd work for nothing just to get the chance to do what you do. I'm as serious as a heart attack."

I watched his face slowly soften into a smile. He said…"call me some evening, at the station. After 5:15. That's my last newscast. If you're serious, I'll help you with the tape."

Now, at this very moment, I am convinced that there is, without doubt, a loving and caring God in Heaven. I can practically hear trumpets playing somewhere. I have heard of miracles , read about them, and I, Ed Friel, have now experienced one. A few days later, I called WCHI. I'd been listening to the station, and had heard Steve do the news. I recognized the voice on the telephone. It was the DJ who had just introduced the Beachboy's hit, Surf City….imagine that! I'm talking directly to a real DJ! I asked for Steve Stevens, terrified I might get the disappointment of my life; that Steve wasn't available….or he'd died….or didn't work there anymore….

"Hang on just a minute" the DJ said." Then… "Stevens" he hollered … "get line 1…and where the hell's the promo for the bowling news?"

Steve came on the line. I told him who I was, reminded him of our talk in the bathroom. Steve said "can you come down here later this evening?" It was a Friday…no school tomorrow, so I said yes (providing, God and the Old Man willing) I can borrow Dad's maroon Nash Ambassador.

"Great, " Steve said."Come down around 8:30. Bang on the door hard, it'll be locked. I have to come back to work the late shift 'til signoff at midnight. You can do the 11:30 news headlines for me. I'll tape that, and that'll be your audition tape."

I'm hearing trumpets again. God is signaling me….Me?? Do the 11:30 news headlines ? Live? On the air? Did I hear that correctly, or am I delirious?? Maybe I just died, and I'm in Heaven.

I asked Dad if I could borrow the car. "What for?", he asked with a frown.

Guess he assumed I was going to meet Roger at Johnnie's Drive Inn, and then cruise out to the Sumburger on U.S. 23 where, rumor was, lots of girls from out in the county 'hot to trot' hung out. So far, the only girl I had ever talked to at the Sumburger, and thought I was making progress, was Mary Kay, a sophomore at CHS. I'd heard about Mary Kay…boy, had I heard about Mary Kay! She was…hot! Even the other girls said, a little scornfully, that she was 'hot to trot'.

What I HADN'T heard was that Mary Kay was dating a Marine. A Marine who happened to be home on leave that particular weekend, and had been in the Sumburger bathroom. He came out, walked straight up to me as I was talking to Mary Kay, (using my best Elvis inflection). He didn't miss a step; just walked up to me and, almost as an afterthought, slapped me with his open hand on the side of my head. I dropped ignomeniously to the pavement, my ears ringing...on my knees, tears beginning to stream, I heard him say "sorry about that insect, Mary Kay, I think I got 'im"

Anyway, I really needed the old Ambassador. "Dad", I said seriously, "I gotta go down to WCHI...you know, the radio station. Steve Stevens wants me to do the 11:30 news"

Now, if I had told my Dad I had just won the Irish Sweepstakes, been made Pope, or that Kim Novak was dropping by for cocktails, he could not possibly have been more surprised. He actually dropped his newspaper, and as his head snapped up to meet my eyes.

"What?? You? News? WCHI?? What in Sam Hill are you talking about? Are you drunk?"

I quickly told Dad the story...wanting to be on radio more than life itself; of meeting Steve Stevens (Steve Stevens is a TEENAGER?? Dad asked increduously). And, of Steve offering me a chance to do an audition tape...live, on the radio. "You mean you'll be on the radio, tonight at 11:30? We'll be able to hear you??"

I told Dad "that's what Steve says"... My Old Man grinned slightly, stood up to get the keys out of his pocket, and handed me a dollar bill. " Better put 3 gallons in the tank before you get too far. darn thing's runnin' on fumes".

Then…"you really going to be on the radio?" I told him it sounded like it. The Old Man just grinned and shook his head.

I drove down to WCHI. The station was in a small one story brick building on the edge of town, with a big red neon "WCHI" out front. There was one car in the parking lot. Talk about excited! I'm about to pee my pants! Here I am, about to walk into a real radio station, with the promise of a chance to sit down in front of a real microphone, and to actually talk to millions…. My little kid's dream is at hand….

I knocked on the front door…hard. Through the glass, I saw Steve emerge from a room on the right. He opened the door and I stepped inside.

"Let me show you around. I've got a network feed on, so we have some time." Man, I thought, that voice coming out of a kid my age.

And I was in my version of Heaven! A real radio station, broadcasting to millions! "Well, actually", Steve said "our signal only goes out about 30 miles," but we're real strong all over town".

My mental picture of the surrounding 30 miles took in a lot of corn fields and rail yards. Okay, so this isn't NBC….but hey, it's the first real radio station I've ever seen! I was like a starving man at a smorgsborg!! Let's get on with the tour!

He showed me the main studio, on the immediate right…a room with a small desk; a microphone (WCHI nameplate on top), a few folding chairs and a piano. There was a glass window behind the desk that looked into the control room. We went down the hall, and stepped inside the control room.

Allllrrriggght….I thought to myself; this is definitely where I want to spend the rest of my life. I took a deep, satisfying breath. I had finally arrived…

I was facing a big console filled with dials, switches, buttons, red lights. On top of the console, a notebook, containing, Steve told me "advertising copy"…

Copy…I thought. A real radio buzzword; gotta use that with the Old Man.

Two huge turntables flanked the console, the announcers chair between the turntables. Behind the chair, a bank of reel to reel tape decks. The microphone was suspended on a flex rod mounted to the wall; it could be raised or lowered, depending if the announcer wanted to sit or stand.

Shelves filled with records lined every available square foot of the walls. Soundproof tiles covered the ceiling, door, and the walls of the main studio, visible through the glass. This was a state of the art, AM radio station, in 1960.

Steve explained the general arrangement, and what the various buttons and dials did. A speaker on the wall monitored the program on the air. Steve glanced at the big clock on the wall above the console, and said "sit over there and don't say anything…I've got to do a station break. " Well, I thought; truly, I have died and gone to Heaven. I am actually going to be in the studio where a REAL Radio Guy is going to do a station break. This is beyond cool. It was, to me, anyway…Steve put on earphones, held up his hand as a signal to be quiet. (Lord, I thought…don't let me sneeze)." Steve flipped a switch, a red light instantly appeared on the console, and Steve spoke into the mike: "WCHI Radio, Chillicothe, Ohio, 1350 on your dial. Stay tuned for the 9:00 pm news from Mutual Radio. He flipped another switch, took off his headset, and said to me "just like a real radio station!"

Heck, this is pretty cool. Steve Stevens joking with me. I was accepted into his world!

I managed to get through the 11:30 news without too many mistakes. Steve ran the board from the control room; I sat at the little desk in the studio, wishing I'd thought to bring my camera. Think how impressed Mary Kay would be to see a picture of me behind this microphone!

Taking no chances , I had called the Old Man from the station office at 11:15 and told him I was really going to be on the air. I could picture Mom and Dad leaning toward the radio as , solemnly, I delivered the news.

Steve promised to get the tape to the Chief Announcer "soon". Why not tomorrow, I thought. I'm ready to go to work NOW.

The days passed. Every day, I'd come home and ask Mom if I'd had any calls. Mom could read the disappointment on my face when she had to tell me "none today...except for Roger..." Crap. Roger's all right, but I'm waiting for Fame to call!

Late one afternoon, after I'd gotten home from school the phone rang. Probably good ol' Roger. "Hey, Rog", I said.

The deep voice on the other end asked for me, by name. My heart leaped....yup...it's Mr. Hughes , from the station. " I've listened to your tape, son." He paused.

"Thank's," I blurted out. "For my first time , I thought it was pretty good" "What you think doesn't matter" he snapped. "Here's the deal. You come in Saturday morning at 4:30. You'll do the 5AM to 7 shift. Curly will be here; you'll do the first two hours of his show. He'll show you the ropes. I'm not gonna pay you for the two hours. If you do okay, we'll talk. If you bomb, your through. Got it? 4:30 AM. Saturday. Don't be late."

WOW! Me? Doing the first two hours of the Curly Miller Show? Curly was only the biggest country and western DJ on Chillicothe radio…a Famous Personality!! The Old Man listened to Curly Miller on his way to work at the Federal prison. Curly was on six days a week, from 5am until 9; then back in from 2 until 5:00. I was not only going to meet this star of Radio; I was going to work with him! Me and THE Curly Miller. We'd become fast friends, I thought. I'd impress my friends when I would introduce them to "my good buddy, Curly Miller. "

I hung up the phone…my hands shaking; in absolute shock. God in Heaven, I've got a CHANCE!

I briefly wondered if this was how Walter Cronkite got started….on a 5 am country music show? Coulda been, I thought to myself.

I had trouble sleeping that Friday night. First, I sat down at the desk my brother John and I shared for homework. " Gotta write my show", I said importantly to Mom and Dad, who just smiled and nodded. Dad had asked me at least a dozen times since the phone call " you REALLY going to be on the radio for two hours??" I think that's the first time I'd ever done anything that impressed the Old Man.

After about an hour, I gave up trying to "write my show". Actually, the only thing Curly did was introduce country records, read commercials, and give time and weather reports….all in a relaxed and raspy drawl. His banter occasionally interrupted by what sounded like a smokers cough.

I tossed and turned in bed….my stomach in a knot of excitement, nervousness; my head swimming with thoughts of tomorrow. Mom had promised to get me up at 3:30 and fix me a nice breakfast before I had to "go to work"!

I left the house at 4:15, Mom fussing with my shirt. "You want to look nice for the audience", she said.

"Mom...it's radio, remember?" Geez.

"I don't care. Mr. Miller will see you, and you want to make a good impression"!

God broke the mold after he made Mom.

I arrived at the radio station at 4:30am. Still dark. The red neon sign with the call letters...MY call letters...WCHI. Behind the station, the tower rose several hundred feet up, topped with a blinking red light. In a half hour , that tower will be beaming my voice across south central Ohio, I thought; wonder if Mary Kay will be listening?

The lights were on in the station, and there was an old pickup truck in the parking lot. Must be Curly's, I reasoned. I parked the maroon Ambassador next to it and got out. I noticed the pickup was missing the left front fender, and a piece of cardboard was duct taped over the passenger window.

I walked through the unlocked door, went inside and down the hall to the control room. Curly (I supposed) was standing in the transmitter room, directly behind the control room, trying to pour coffee into a mug. His hands were shaking so badly that coffee was spilling onto the shelf that held a hotplate, and dripping onto the floor. "Curly Miller?" I asked.

I must have startled him.

"HOLY SHIT!" he screamed, jerking the coffee cup, coffee sloshing out in all directions. He slammed the cup down on the counter and turned around unsteadily to see who had come in , shaking his left hand in pain from the hot coffee he'd spilled. "I'm sorry, Mr. Miller! I didn't mean to scare you!" Crapcrapcrap. Just what I needed. A rocky start with the star of Chillicothe radio.

"Ah hell, boy" he said, still shaking his hand to ease the pain" Don't worry about it. Guess I'm a little jumpy. Didn't get to bed last night. Hell, I just left the card game about an hour ago." He reached back to his cup on the counter, and held it in his shaking right hand. Curly was a little shorter than me, in spite of the scuffed high heel cowboy boots he wore. His worn jeans were faded; traces of grease and coffee stains on them. He wore an old blue plaid shirt with a yellowed undershirt showing at the neck, and a well-worn black cowboy hat. With at least three days growth of scragily gray beard, he could have been 35 or 65. He took stock of me, his bloodshot eyes staring out from behind thick glasses. Scotch tape held the left ear piece to the frame.

He turned back to refill his coffee, carefully holding the hot pot. I walked on into the control room, and that's when I got a whiff of Curly…a sour combination of beer, cigarettes, sweat; and clothes that definitely hadn't been near soap and water in a long time.

Curly turned to me, and said " I'm glad you're here, son. You'll give me a chance to catch a few winks on the couch in the office. Ol' Hank William's his ownself never had a hangover like I got right now ….not after his longest night of drinkin'. Wake me up during the 7 o'clock news." He started out of the control room towards the small front office; stopped in the hallway, lifted his left foot…and farted, an ominous, bubbly fart. Then continued unsteadily into the office.

"Uh….Mr. Miller " I said uncertainly. "This is my first time on the radio. I've never done this before"

He stopped, dead still. He stood there, his back to me, and then shook his head. He turned slowly;squinting his bloodshot eyes to focus on me.

"You gotta be shittin' me, boy….you ain't never done this? This is your first time? You don't even know how to run the board?"

He shook his head in disgust. "Hell, they didn't tell me you was a complete greenhorn." I stammered an apology. "I'm sorry, Mr. Miller…I really am."

He cut me off with a snort and another shake of his head. "Guess it serves me right. Hell, I won about $23 dollars playin' poker last night. Spent ever cent and then some on Pabst Blue Ribbon….and a few shots of Jack. Guess you're just the Lord's way of puttin' me in my place."

He sighed, shook his head again, and said, "well come on. Lemme show you how to turn on the transmitter. Damn…my head is gonna explode."

He showed me the 6 switches that needed to be turned on to allow the huge transmitter to warm up…"we'll punch the 7th one right at 5" he said…."turn it on before 5 o'clock, and those ol' boys down to the FCC office get their shorts in a knot"…

Then he gave me a lesson on 'runnin' the board'. Which switches did what; how to cue records on the big turntables so the song started as soon as the button was pushed. "The Boss will jump yore tail if he hears any dead air. Don't let thet happen!"

Several times Curly got close enough that I got a direct blast of his breath. If the folks from Webster had been in the room, they'd have gone into immediate re-write mode on the definition of halitosis…adding a lot more adjectives and exclamation points!

Now it was 4:56…four minutes until showtime. Curly showed me how to cue the tape of the National Anthem "We always start the day with that song" he said solemnly.

At 4:59, Curly sat down in a folding chair he'd set up close to turntable 1, (the one on the left). "Okay, boy….go hit that big red button on the transmitter, then come back in here and start the National Anthem. When it ends, hit the stop button, and read that intro"…his gnawed and callused finger pointed shakily to the big 3 ring binder on top of the console, opened to the first page.

The second hand on the big wall clock swept past 5:00am. I hit the tape button, and the sounds of the recorded Anthem filled the room….the needle on the VU meter in the center of the board bouncing back and forth. My heart was pounding; my legs jiggling rapidly, my breathing shallow…throat tight. Would I be able to get the words out? Were Mom and Dad hearing the National Anthem, their hearts bursting with pride? Was my brother John….forget it. John wouldn't get up unless the Little Rascals were on tv. Wait! Maybe Mary Kay is stirring in her bed at this very moment, and will jolt upright when she hears my voice…her heart yearning for me.

The anthem ended…and I started to read, my normally deep voice high-pitched and shaking.

"Good morning. This is WCHI, 1350 on your dial" Out of the corner of my eye, I could see Curly raise his eyes Heavenward. Then he slowly stood up, leaned over the turntable and put his hand on the mike switch.

He fixed me with his rheamy, bloodshot eyes and with a tired sigh said "Main thing about radio, Ace, is always make sure you turn on your microphone before you start to talk" He switched on the mike with his right hand; with his left, he pointed back to the beginning of the intro, then slumped back into his chair, groaning slightly and burying his face in his hands.

"Good morning" I started again. "This is WCHI….."

The two hours passed with a heart stopping disaster for me every couple of minutes. "Where's the Ford commercial, Curly!"…."damn, wrong George Jones cut…sorry, Curly"….where do I find the 5:30 news stuff, Curly?"….the record's stuck! What now, Curly?"….Crap, Curly, I cue'd Hank Snow to a hymn instead of Honky Tonk Momma." And so on.

Thank God for the numbing effects of alcohol. Curly took it all in stride, much like a patient pet owner with a new, untrained puppy. More than once, he reached over to find the right page in the big 3 ring binder; cue'd a record for me…or pointed to the right button to push. His halitosis was starting to have the soothing affect of a mother's soft assurance. Think of the catastrophe this would be without him!

Finally, it was 7 o'clock. I read the intro for the Mutual Network news, and flipped the switch that put the network feed on the air.

I sat back, and looked over at Curly. His head was drooping, a soft, wet snore just barely audible.

"Curly, I can't thank you enough for putting up with me. I hope I get another chance"

Curly looked up; took off his hat and scratched his head through matted hair, then put the hat back on.

"Hell, boy; we all gotta start sometime and someplace" He stood up, lifted his left leg, and farted again….this time, a less threatening sound…

"Sometime, I'll tell you about my first job," he yawned, standing slowly and scratching his crotch.

We exchanged places. I wanted to stick around and see a professional in action. And, Curly was just that. When the news ended, he started the theme music for "The Curly Miller Show." (I made a mental note to find some theme music for "The Easy Ed Show" which, in my fantasies, I would have soon). Curly lapsed into the friendly, raspy banter that endeared him to fans across south central Ohio, mixing the latest country hits with a smooth flow of commercials, weather tips, hog reports; his callused fingers playing the control board effortlessly. Not a second of dead air….not a moment of panic. He was smooth; a real pro.

The control room door opened just after 8am. A short, stocky and balding man wearing dress slacks and an open necked, white, short sleeved shirt entered. He stuck out his hand. "Don Hughes", he said.

I jumped up. Don Hughes!! He did sports on the air, and Steve had told me he was the Chief Announcer! My stomach knotted…my shoulders tightened. My fate was in his hands. Please, God…please.

"Gimme a minute with Curly, will you, kid?" he said , motioning me to step out. He closed the door. I walked toward the front door; from the corner of my eye I could see Mr. Hughes through the control room window, talking seriously to Curly. Curly was leaning back in the chair, his hands behind his head, a Bill Anderson tear-jerker coming from the hall speakers. Hughes' face was expressionless as he listened to what ever Curly was saying.

Finally Hughes nodded and started to open the door to come out into the hallway. He walked up to me put his hands on his hips and looked me square in the eye. I swallowed…my heart pounding.

"Curly says you did okay, kid. If you still want the job, it's yours. Pays a dollar an hour. You'll be low man on the totem pole, so you take the hours I give you, when I need you. Can you start tomorrow?"

God in Heaven. I wanted to drop to the floor and kiss his shoes. Could I start tomorrow?? I can start right now!! Why wait??" But I said, "thank you Mr. Hughes. I am honored with the offer. I certainly can start tomorrow. Thank you." We shook hands and he turned to go into his office. "Be here at noon" he said over his shoulder. "You'll work with one of the other part-timers until 5:00. Make sure you pay attention. Next time, you'll be on your own. Nobody to wet nurse you".

I floated out to the car....couldn't wait to get home to see the expression in the Old Man's eyes when I told him I was the new announcer for WCHI, 1350 on your dial.

Mary Kay, eat your heart out!

I got all the rotten hours, but I didn't care. 5:00 am until 5:00pm every Sunday. 5:00am until 7:00am on Saturdays. "Curly wants to cut back on weekends", Mr. Hughes told me.

And later, as I got more experience, 4:00pm until 8:00pm weekdays. I'd leave Chillicothe High School after my last class; drive to the station, and become "Easy Ed" from 4 until 8, playing rock and roll on my own radio show. I was in Hog Heaven.

Sundays were the most profitable day the station had. Chillicothe was in the middle of the Bible belt, and the station happily sold time to any of the hundreds of small, church's or preachers who had the money. Fifteen dollars for fifteen minutes. Twenty seven fifty for a half hour. And, sure, we'll sell you a full hour...that'll be $56 bucks.

The radio log for the each day's programming was typed on 8 ½ x 14 paper. It listed everything that was to go on the air, with times; news on the hour and half hour, weather, bowling news, hog reports, and commercials. Paid commercials were typed in red. On Sundays, the entire log was typed in red. Every hour was sold, mostly in fifteen or thirty minute segments.

Some of the church programs were taped, but many were live. Mostly, these were small Pentecostal churches with self anointed "pastors"….Pastor Al, Pastor Hubert. These folks would come to the station to do their program, often bringing a piano player, singers, wives, kids ,etc. Sometimes I'd have as many as thirty people milling around in the hall, waiting to go on, while another group would be in the studio, on the air.

Sundays turned the station into a nuthouse. Nervous first time preachers pacing the hall, sometimes wandering into the control room, despite the "Strictly No Admittance" sign; others staring in wonder through the control room window. My job was to run the board for the various programs from the control room; I'd introduce the program, then open the mike in the studio. From then until the end of that program, I'd monitor the VU meter, collect money from the incoming preachers, try to keep order in the hall; all while watching the clock. I had to get the Church of The Bleeding Hands of Jesus off the air by 9:58, so that the Full Gospel Church of Loaves and Fish's from East Nosebleed, Ohio could go on at 10:00. Two minutes for one group to leave the studio, and another group to set up, while I did a station break. It was like herding cockroach's.

Most of the time, after introducing one of the church groups, I'd listen for a minute or so, then switch the speakers from"Air Monitor" to "cue", and put a rock record on the turntable. I'd listen to Buddy Holly, while Pastor Barney or whoever railed against sin and fornication. Occasionally, I'd glanced at the meters to be sure the good pastor hadn't accidently knocked himself off the air.

During one of the afternoon programs, I had Duane Eddy on the speakers. There was a group of probably fifteen sweating people in the studio; a bald guy in a plaid shirt mouthing into the microphone. I hadn't been listening to him; just groovin to Rebel Rouser. The light on the control room phone lit up. Probably my favorite girl at the time. "WCHI", I answered in my best Radio Announcer voice. It was my Dad.

"Eddie, are you listening to that guy you got on the radio?"

" Uh, no....haven't checked him for a few minutes. Why"

"Eddie, that's the worst stuff I've ever heard. You better listen to what he saying...it's awful."

I immediately switched the speaker to "air". "You heard me right, all of you out there in radioland...HUH! The end is right around the corner...but I am your Salvation! HUH! Send $5 to Pastor Woodrow in care of this station...HUH!...and I'll send you a genuine, bloodstained piece of wood taken from the Cross of Jesus...HUH! I guarentee it's the real thing...HUH! For $10 dollars I'll guarantee you a seat in Glorious Heaven at the foot of God Himself...HUH! The phone lit up again. This time it was Mr. Hughes...

"Friel, take that jerk off the air ....NOW! And get 'em out of the station. But make sure you get the money he owes for today. Put some hymns on or something"

"Yes, Mr. Hughes. I've been concerned about his pitch. I was just about to call you."

Thank God for the Old Man.

"Just get 'em outta there". He hung up.

I killed the studio mike and started an album of hymns by Tennessee Ernie Ford. (The Old Man liked Tennessee Ernie…he'll be pleased) I thought. Pastor Woodrow didn't notice the "On Air" light had blinked off in the studio for a second. When he did, I was already marching my 17 year old skinny butt past the 2:00pm group in the hall (from the Rosebud, Ohio Church of the Bloody Nails) and into the studio to "throw that jerk out".

I opened the studio door. "What's goin' on? Is my mike off? " Pastor Woodrow asked.

"Yup….the Boss called. Ordered me to take you off the air" Tennessee Ernie was just starting "Take My Hand Precious Lord" when the good pastor erupted.

"%$#@!, I paid for this *%^&$ half hour, and want you to put me back on the #@$%! air," he hollered.

" Sorry. It ain't my call. I'm just hired help. Now, I gotta ask you to leave. Oh, yeah; the Boss says to get the twenty seven fifty you owe"

The color drained from Pastor Woodrow's face. " You little $#@! You can tell your Boss to kiss my God fearing $#! I ain't payin' you &*%!" He pushed past me and motioned his entourage to follow.

Looking back, Pastor Woodrow made Jim and Tammy Faye look downright respectable.

Helen O'Connor was the class act of WCHI. A distinguished woman in her early 60's, I suppose. She had a one hour daily program from 11:00 until noon. She had guests from around the area, recipes, advice for daily life, and her program was sponsored by the local phone company. Helen made the station a lot of money. Helen did her show from the studio, rather than from the control room. . Seated at the small desk, behind the microphone. She had no interest in learning the complexities of the control board. That meant that one of the other announcers had to run the board for her.There was a window between the studio and the control room; Helen's desk was at the window, so that she faced into the control room.

One of Helen's requests was that whoever was running the board should stay seated at the board and not move around the control room. It made her nervous, she said. She wanted to be sure that she could immediately get attention if something went wrong.

The engineer had installed a 'cough button' on Helen's mike, so that if she had to cough, she could kill the mike herself. Invariabily, when she coughed, she would always say "excuse me" when she turned the mike back on. The listener would hear a few seconds of silence, then "excuse me".

One of the full time air personalities for a time was John, who followed Curly's show. John had board duty from 9:00am until 4; that mean't he had Helen's program to handle. John absolutely hated doing Helen's show. The first few days, after putting Helen on the air, John would go into the DJ lounge across the hall to relax or get a coke. He'd wander around the control room, selecting records for his show, or reading Playboy. That drove Helen nuts. She complained to Mr. Hughes. John didn't have a chance, since Helen was the source of much of the sponsor money that made up the station's revenue.

So John seethed at the board, while pretending to be enjoying every minute of Helen's show (John had learned Mr. Hughes was not someone you wanted in your face twice on the same issue). But John had a plan. He told me one day he was going to do it. I thought it sounded like a sure fire way to get fired. But that didn't faze John.

The next day, I learned later, John carried out his plan....and was fired before Helen's show was over. Helen was in the midst of an interview with a guest when John, watching from the control room , saw her press her cough button. At that instant, John hit the tape "play" button….and the massive fart he had taped earlier was broadcast all over south central Ohio. The next thing Helen's large audience heard was her sweet, almost musical voice, saying "excuse me".

The station secretary told me Mr. Hughes went into the control room, escorted John out of the building and fired him, paying him through the end of Helen's show. She also said that Hughes and John were laughing heartily in the parking lot, where John's car was already loaded with all his belongings.

Most DJ's at small town stations in those days drifted from station to station, seldom staying longer than six months, always looking for a bigger and better gig. So, for John, this was just a wonderfully memorable way to say goodbye to Chillicothe, and to Helen O'Connor; then head down the road to the next small town with a radio station, one step closer, hopefully, to a distant shot at the 'big time'.

Mr. Hughes was in the front office one afternoon with the station secretary, going over the next day's log. It was around 3:30; I'd just gotten out of school and was due to go on the air for "The Easy Ed Show " at 4 o'clock. He looked up as I walked in, and said "some guy just called for you. From the Rotary Club. They want you to be their guest speaker at lunch next week."

I'd probably been working at WCHI for about six months by this time. I'd had my own regular show from 4-8 weekdays for about 3 months, and usually worked most of the day Saturday, and all day Sunday, loving every minute of it.

"The Rotary Club? What's that?" I asked. "It's a businessmans club, stupid. Everybody's heard of the Rotary Club. They meet every month, down at the Hotel". He handed me a scrap of paper with the name 'Matt Lynn' and a phone number.

"Here's the guys name. Give'im a call" He turned back to his work.

I had some time before going on the air. I went in the control room, said "hi" to Bill who would be getting off at 4, and went into the DJ lounge to make the call.

"Mr. Lynn? Ed Friel...WCHI Radio". (In my best Radio Announcer voice.)

"Mr. Friel! Thank you for calling. It's an honor to speak to you" he said in a voice twinged with excitement...

An honor to speak to me? What the heck?

He continued " We'd like for you to be the speaker at our lunch meeting next week. Talk about what it's like to work in radio; a little about your life before coming to WCHI". Fine by me, I thought. Wonder if I can get a pass to get out of school for a couple of hours? Hey, this is the Rotary Club. Surely Mr. Wiley would let me speak to the Rotary Club.

So I said "Mr. Lynn, I am delighted to accept". We discussed the time and place to meet, and I hung up right after saying "see you at the Hotel at 11:30".

The following Monday, I wore a suit to school. My pal Roger and several other guys razed me mercilessly. "Where you preachin', Reverend"; and "you sure look purty in that red tie....you steal it from your Old Man?" I left school and drove downtown in the snazzy '52 Ford I'd bought from Steve Stevens for $300. Found a place to park and walked up the granite steps of the hotel. There…a sign that said Rotary Club lunch, with an arrow pointing down the hall.

I walked into the meeting room. About 10 big round tables, each seating 8 Rotarians. So far, about 30 businessmen, most dressed in suits, were scattered among the tables. At the front of the room, the Head Table and, centered on the table, the lectern with the Rotarian seal. Two men were standing near the head table; one of them, I reasoned, had to be my new friend and fan, Mr. Lynn.

I walked up to them. They continued their conversation. Hmm, I thought…must be pretty important. I stood there expectantly, waiting for a break in the conversation. Heck, they were just talking about golf, and they continued to ignore me. After about five minutes, I said "excuse me."

Both men now turned to me, looking mildly irritated at being interrupted.

"Whaddya want, kid?", one of them asked…

"I'm looking for Mr. Lynn. I'm Ed Friel". Both men reacted as if they'd been slapped. Their jaws dropped, and for some reason, that seemed funny; just like in the movies.

"YOU!! YOU'RE ED FRIEL??? How the hell old are you, anyway?" the taller man asked, shaking his head in disbelief.

I told him; "seventeen, sir. I'm a senior at CHS." "Seventeen? I can't believe this! You sure you're Ed Friel, the radio Ed Friel?" asked the man, who I now assumed was Mr. Lynn.

I assured him I was, indeed, Ed Friel of WCHI Radio. His face seemed to soften slightly as he recognized my voice.

"Hell, Ed, forgive me for being shocked. We all figured with that voice, you had to be at least 50 years old, and tip the scales at 250 pounds!"

Yup, I thought to myself, Mom told everyone that even my cry was deeper than the other babies in the hospital.

My radio career continued through high school and college. WCHI and WBEX in Chillicothe, and brief stints at stations in Jackson, Ohio and Welch, West Virginia. If I'd stayed with it, who knows what might have happened. But, when I got out of Ohio State, reality told me it was time to find a real job. I'd gotten married to my childhood sweetheart during my senior year at Ohio State and, hormones being what they are, I quickly had not only a wife, but also a mother and child to support and care for. So I needed a job that paid real money, instead of minimum wage, which was the norm back then in small town radio.

Most of the DJ's I had worked with also did what I did. They lived their fantasy for a brief while, then followed the money. A few stayed with radio and a few of those even made it to major markets. But radio is a career dependent on "the past six months ratings" as one friend put it, just before he lost his afternoon drive time show in Upstate New York.

I recently took a tour of a "state of the art" radio station. Talk about disappointment! No turntables. No tape decks. Just a bank of computers. And a mike. Not one of the classic microphones like at WCHI, WBEX, or NBC, either. Hell, that "state of the art" studio mike could have come from Radio Shack. And, everybody and their brother has a computer these days. So, what's the big deal about seeing a radio station?

I'm glad I was there when a radio studio was something special, something unique, something boys built up into fantasies, and that I actually got to live it out, to make it part of my reality and now part of my memory.

Chapter 6

Make Mine a Screaming Orgasm, Please

Agnes and me with my diploma from the Colorado School of
Bartending

It was supposed to be a typical Friday evening event after a long week at work. My wife and I would have a glass of wine after we got home from work, then take a short drive to one of our favorite restaurants in the Littleton suburb of Denver. On this particular evening, the restaurant was busy, and the maitre d' suggested we have a drink in the bar while we waited for a table.

There is something comforting and homey about a well appointed bar. Rich woodwork. Comfortable furniture. Background music. The soft confusion of voices in a hundred different conversations. People relaxing. People having a good time. And, at the center of it all… the Bartender.

The Bartender! If this were the New York Philharmonic, he'd be Leonard Bernstein. If this were Metropolis, he'd be Superman.

The Bartender. Orchestrating the evening for his fans. In control. At the center of things. Admired. Envied. Everyone wanting to be his friend. To be on a first name basis with the Bartender was to have Arrived.

"Look at that guy," I said to my wife, as I swirled the remains of a perfect Rob Roy in its stemmed glass. "He's got the best job in the world. Works in a great environment, meets tons of interesting people, has fun, and is the Father Confessor to any number of people who come in here to forget their problems."

At the time, I was a middle level manager for a distribution company in Denver. Maybe the least satisfying job I ever had. "I think, in my next life, I'm gonna be a bartender," I said absently, leaning back in my chair.

Two weeks later, it was Christmas. There, in my Christmas stocking, was a gift certificate to attend Abby's School of Bartending.

Several weeks later, I stopped in at the Bartending School. It was on the first floor of a corner building on Colorado Boulevard, with a picture window looking out on the street. Inside, it was just like a real working bar. Several young people were behind the bar, making drinks and looking over small recipe books. A handsome, self-confident Hispanic man walked up to me with a smile and asked if he could help me. This was Abby, I guessed.

Abby told me he owned the school. I told him about my gift certificate, and he explained how the school operated. It was a six week course on drink mixing, beer and wine, and some bar business management. He said most of his students were young people who were looking for their first jobs, who thought bartending was an easy and fun way to make a living.

I told him I had a job, and wasn't interested in a career change. I just wanted to see what bartending was like. And I could only attend evening classes, since I worked full time.

"No problem, man," he said. "You come when you can. You'll meet a lot of interesting people here. You'll have a lot of fun. Plus, you can make some money on the side. You got a tux shirt and bow tie?"

"Sure," I said, curious.

"We get lots of calls here at the school for bartenders for private parties," he said. "The run of the mill parties I give to the students. The interesting parties, the upscale ones, I take myself. You're an older guy. You'll fit in better as a bartender at those parties. You want, you can work with me on the good ones." "Sounds good to me," I told Abby. Heck, maybe John Elway would be throwing a party soon. Wondered what he drinks?

I started taking classes, two hours on those evenings when I could attend. Abby let me be flexible. In fact, flexibility defined the school. It was low key, almost a party atmosphere. Abby believed in having fun with his work. We worked with bottles of colored water to represent the various liquors. Occasionally, we'd have a "live class," in which we used the real stuff. If he was teaching us to make some colorful layered drink, colored water wouldn't work. Had to use the real thing. Making a layered drink was tricky. You had to put the heavier liquors in first, then carefully layer the other lighter liquors so they would float on top without mixing. While Abby said there wasn't much call for layered drinks, they were fun to make and profitable. You could charge a lot of money for a seven or eight-layered drink.

We learned free pouring- how to pour a precise 2 ounces without using a shot glass. (It's all in the timing.) And speed mixing, so we could keep up with the demands of a hot bar. We memorized recipes.

About three weeks into school, as I walked in one evening, Abby came up to me and said, "We got a party, man; you and me. The Hispanic Policeman's Association. I bartended it once before, man. It's a happening party."

It was on a Saturday night, a week off. Abby said we'd each get $100 for 3 hours, plus tips. "Cops tip good, man. Cops and firemen. They're the best. They got a dangerous job, man. When they party, they relax, and have a good time. We'll make some serious money."

Saturday night came. Abby and I met at the school, and stocked up with our tools, corkscrews, shot glasses, towels, knives and fruit for garnishes. Abby had a name tag for me, a white plastic name tag that said ED. Under that, in smaller letters, Abby's School of Bartending.

The party was at a hall in west Denver. As we set up our bars, people began arriving; officers and their dates, husbands, wives…dressed to the nine's and ready to party.

The Hispanic Police Association was made up of all the Mexican-American police officers in the Denver area. At each bar, the Association had provided an officer to help pour beer, so we could concentrate on mixed drinks. I set up my bar, not far from Abby's, introduced myself to the officer helping with beer, and got ready for MY FIRST BARTENDING EXPERIENCE! I had my recipe book out of sight, but handy, just in case. I didn't want to embarrass myself on my first job. The music started. A south of the border band. My first customer approached. A short young woman in a dazzling red dress.

"What may I get for you ?" I asked with my best and most confident bartender voice.

"I would like a Yellow Bird. Make it a double," she said.

Ahh crap, I thought helplessly. My mind was blank. What in blazes was in a Yellow Bird? I fumbled for my little recipe book, my hands shaking. More people were lining up to order, and my first customer was shifting from foot to foot, in time with the band.

I flipped through the book. Yellow Bird. Where the hell is the recipe?

"Hey man, let's go!!" I looked up. Several impatient (and obviously thirsty) customers, wanted to be served…. now.

I forced a smile to the short woman. "Just a minute, ma'am…be right back!" I had to get to Abby to see what the hell was in a Yellow Bird. I eased quickly over to his bar. Abby was clearly in his element; swiftly and smoothly pouring drinks, bantering with his customers, and I could see his tip jar was already brimming.

"Abby, what the hell is a Yellow Bird? My first customer wants a Yellow Bird!!"

Abby didn't miss a beat as he continued to mix drinks, two at a time. He said, "Tell her you don't got the stuff for a Yellow Bird. Make her a double vodka with lime and a little tonic. And for God's sake, get that panic off your face! Smile! This is a party. Get 'em happy! Serve 'em what you got; gin, vodka, whisky, wine. This ain't the The Broadmoor."

My face red, I went quickly back to my bar, where a group of impatient customers waited. I made a strong Vodka tonic, threw in a lime slice, and handed it to the lady in red. "Close as I can come to a Yellow Bird," I said with an uncertain smile.

"Thank you Ed," she said, dropping a dollar in my tip glass, and heading back to her table.

Well crap, why didn't I think of that myself? Why panic in front of Abby? Just make 'em a drink! Make 'em anything, as long as it's close.

"Yours?" I asked the next person, hoping they'd ask for a Cosmopolitan. Just to try my newfound ingenuity. I knew now how to handle any request.

One of my next customers was a young, handsome man in a brown three piece suit. Tie knotted perfectly. Black hair combed just so.

"I'll have a martini, please. Gin. Very dry. A double. Not too much ice."

I took pains to make a perfect martini. After all, this fellow was probably a detective, one of Denver's finest. I sneaked a look to see if his jacket bulged where, undoubtedly, he carried a gun in a shoulder holster. I didn't see anything. Maybe he was wearing an ankle holster, I thought.

During the evening, he came back to my bar several times. Each time with the same order. Martini. Gin. Very dry. A double. This guy was drinking a lot of gin. Gin is very powerful stuff. And, each time he came up, he was just a little less put together.

Around eleven o'clock, he was back. This time, his tie was loosened. His shirt was open at the neck. And he'd spilled some yellowish something on his shirt. His hair spray had yielded to the heat and humidity. Damp strands of hair fell over his forehead. His eyes were bloodshot, and he struggled to focus on me.

"Mertooni. Die Dubuh.

Good Lord, I thought; this guy is about one sip away from being falling down, gutter crawlin,' commode-huggin' drunk. And he's a cop! I can't serve him! What if he leaves here and has a wreck? I'll be sued. Abby will be sued. I'll lose my real job.

I took his glass, added just a few drops of gin, and tried to reach for some water to add to it, but he was determined. His hand clamped around my wrist, and he positioned the gin bottle over his glass and filled it. He smiled at me crookedly, turned, and staggered away. I watched him until he disappeared into the crowd, then turned to the police officer helping me behind the bar. He was leaning against the wall, sipping on a beer.

"What the heck happens to that guy when he leaves here? What if he gets stopped by the police on the way home? Do you guys have some code that keeps you out of trouble?"

The officer took a sip of his beer, smiled slightly and said, "Nope. That's why I'm working a desk job these days. I left this party last year with a snoot full, and got pulled over on I-25 by a Colorado State Trooper. I got out my badge and ID, handed it to him, but he just looked at it and said, 'You're a cop! You ought to know better!' I spent a night in jail, and lost my license for a year."

I had been thinking about having a little something myself as the party wore on, but the thought of having my wife drive me to work for a year was all the incentive I needed to have another cup of that delicious instant decaf.

The party ended finally, and Abby and I cleaned up our bar area, pocketed our tips, and went to a Denny's to, as he put it, "settle up." We pooled the cash from our tip jars. Over $300! Abby smiled and said, "Not bad, man. Cops are the best. Good tippers. They respect the working man. We split down the middle."

Abby was a class guy. He could have insisted on the bulk of the tip money as the owner, and as my teacher.

Abby was right about cops being good tippers. In fact, as I continued to work parties with Abby, I discovered that the average working guy (or gal) is more generous with tips than many so-called high rollers.

Abby and I worked a reception at the Denver Art Museum some months later, attended by the "movers and shakers" of Denver: oil executives, doctors, lawyers, wives and girl friends. Even the Mayor was there. It was an opportunity for community leaders and wanna-bees to see and be seen. Two things struck me that night at the Art Museum. Executive types approached the bar , laughing and talking among each other. But when they addressed me or Abby, the look on their faces changed slightly- just enough to communicate that we were hired help. We were only there to serve them, quickly, so they could get back to their party. Most took their drinks and turned immediately away from us. With seldom even a "thank you," they turned back to whomever they considered important at the moment.

What they lacked in manners was matched by their stinginess with tips. Maybe the mortgage on the mansion in Cherry Hills, the BMW payment and Junior's private school tuition was keeping these guys awake at night.

But that first night, after the Policeman's party, I drove home almost giddy. What a great experience! I was a BARTENDER (got my own nametag to prove it). Despite the rocky start with the Yellow Bird, I'd had fun, and I was going home with just over $150 bucks. Pretty good money for almost nothing; just like that Dire Straits song said.

Abby called me late one Saturday afternoon.

"Hey, man, how'd you like to make serious money and be in the company of some great looking women?"

I hesitated. After all, I was a married man, the father of two teenagers, and probably not the kind of bait that "great looking women" would fall for.

"Uh Abby, you ain't exactly talkin' to Hugh Hefner here. What do you have in mind?"

Abby laughed. "Hey, loosen up! I scheduled one of the students to bartend for the Denver Models meeting tonight, but he called me. He's sick. He can't make it. This is a party for all the fashion models in Denver. It should be a blast. Want to do it?"

Do I want to bartend for all the fashion models in Denver? Bartend for a group of beautiful women, in skimpy mini-dresses and trendy boots? Some of whom might like the idea of getting to know a mature, balding, bartender? Does a hobbyhorse have a hickory dick? Of course I'd like to do it!

"Well, Abby, I had some plans," (didn't want to seem too anxious) "but I'd be glad to help out."

He gave me the details. A fashion photographer was hosting the party in his loft apartment in downtown Denver. All the coolest and 'in demand ' models would be there. I'd be working alone. Standard fee- $100 bucks. And I'd keep all the tips. Plus, this was a 'society' event; a big deal each year.

The apartment where the party was held was on the 4th floor of a refurbished downtown warehouse. Most of the entire floor was an open living/dining area, with a built in wet bar on one side. The big windows provided a great view of downtown.

The host briefed me on the party. Most of the male and female fashion models got together once a year to network, brag about their upcoming gigs, and drink. As I was setting up, I looked around...and decided I had, indeed, died and gone straight to heaven. Beautiful women everywhere- long dresses, mini skirts, fabulous figures. Not a dog in the pack. I'd have to really thank Abby for this opportunity. Maybe even split the tips with him.

Models tend to drink foo-foo drinks, if that evening was representative of their tastes. Cosmopolitans and the like. But, as a seasoned bartender, I now knew how to handle those requests, and keep my customers satisfied. "Sorry, Ma'am, our host has provided me with just the basics. I don't have the ingredients for a Screaming Orgasm; how about a Screwdriver?"

Works every time.

Later in the evening, one of the male models came sweeping up to the bar, a beautiful girl on each arm. He was dressed in a tux, replete with bow tie and a stiff pointed collar. He had chosen his best white tennis shoes to round out his outfit. His blond hair was swept back in ducktails. He was stunning, a legend in his own mind.

He looked at my name tag and, head tilted upward slightly to in an attitude of superiority, said, "Ed, my good man…can you make me a perfect JB and soda? And find a fine white wine for my companions?"

The two girls were clearly fascinated by their Man Of The World, based on the admiring smiles they gave him, and the look in their eyes that said 'isn't he just TOO fascinating? Tux, for his part, glanced around the big room to see whom he should be schmoozing next.

My cynical side was instantly alert. This jerk wouldn't know J & B scotch from the cheapest bourbon whiskey on the planet, I thought to myself.

So I said, "You bet, Sport. A perfect J & B scotch coming right up. And I have a special bottle of wine for the ladies."

While Tux preened his slicked back hair and bantered with the girls, I fixed him a strong Jim Beam bourbon with soda, and presented it to him with a flourish. "There you are, Sir. A perfect J&B and soda. You really know your scotch, sir!

Tux swirled his drink under his nose, then took a long and critical sip under the admiring stares of his ladies. A smile crossed his face. He bowed to me grandly, and pronounced that drink to be the finest scotch to ever pass his lips. I made him at least two more strong bourbons as the evening wore on. He bragged to his friends all evening that his good friend Ed was undoubtedly the finest bartender who'd ever served him; a man who really knew how to present Scotch whisky as it was meant to be consumed.

Man, this was a great gig.

I even bartended for a coven of witches.

When I moved to Denver I had to find a dentist. In the dental office a friend had recommended, I struck up a conversation with the hygienist.

"What do you do when you aren't being a hygienist?" I asked, in what I thought was my best relationship-building voice.

She gave me a quizzical look, and then looked away, as if deep in thought. She was a striking beauty; tall, long black hair, great figure, and piercing green eyes. She turned back to me.

"Actually, I'm a Witch."

I was instantly alert. I had read articles in Time about witches. Witches who slew cows in Wyoming, and reportedly drank their blood. Witches who danced naked around candles in East Village basements. And pledged their allegiance to Satan, or the Hugo, or some equally horrible menace to the human race.

I hoped she was into the latter. Who wants a witch with blood breath?

She smiled at what must have been my shock. "I'm a Priestess in the Church of Guidea. Don't be offended or put off," she smiled. "I'm a good witch. My name is Gretchen."

I decided immediately I'd second that. There was simply NO QUESTION she was a "GOOD" witch.

She turned those intense eyes on me. "And, what do you do when you aren't my patient?" She smiled slightly, brushing a strand of that beautiful hair away from her face.

I told her I was in the diesel engine business (did I notice her eyes beginning to glaze?), that I also wrote country and western songs, and I was a bartender on the side.

Those great eyes! At the mention of bartending, her eyes came alive, and she flashed a smile.

"Really? A bartender? Our Coven has a Gathering coming up. The Mother High Priestess will be there. We have invited Eduardo to speak. He's a recognized expert on our Church history. And we do need a bartender for the time preceding our Mentoring Session with Eduardo.

We worked out the details. The hotel, where they had arranged a meeting room, the time and, of course, my fee.

Heck, I would have done this one gratis. The Priestess, dancing naked, would have been fee enough.

The day of the Gathering, I arrived at the hotel an hour early. If there was going to be a lot of nudity involved, I wanted to have all my set-ups ready, and my bar stocked, so I could devote my total attention to the activities at hand. All in the interest of a better intellectual understanding of the culture, of course.

I found the room. Rats. Just a standard hotel meeting room. Set up theatre style. With a podium at the front and the bar over to one side. No black candles burning. No strange symbols. Hell, this looked like the Rotary might arrive at any minute. And, if anybody did get naked, those metal chairs were going to be a tad uncomfortable.

I started setting up my bar; arranging the glasses and bottles, slicing lemons and limes for the inevitable gin and tonics, and opening small bottles of cherries and olives for Manhattans and Martinis. I looked up. An older woman in a sensible black dress was approaching. Her hair was in a beehive, and she wore thick glasses straight out of a '50s TV show; with black frames that swooped up, giving her an owl-like look.

She extended her hand. "Hello. I'm Glenda. I am the Mother High Priestess. And you are?"

I introduced myself, as my spirits dropped. This was a Witch? The Boss Witch? The Mother ...whatever? If this old bat decided to get naked, I'd personally call 911. The sight of her wrinkled, sagging butt could have incited a riot.

Others began to arrive. An assortment of women and men. Mostly under forty, and most a tad overweight. All were dressed as if they'd just left work at the bank or office building. Over there, a nurse in blue scrubs. Around the room, small groups talked quietly and intently And just coming in, two young women who were probably college students. Behind them, Gretchen, my Gretchen, walked in accompanied by a tall thin black man carrying a backpack, wearing khakis, sandals, and a red golf shirt.

Must be the famous Eduardo, I thought. This was turning out to be a major bust as a memorable bartending gig- before it even got started. These people were witches? Hell, the Chess Club probably had more bewitching and exciting parties than this.

People started drifting over to my bar. I had on my bartending best- crisp white shirt, black bow tie, my snazzy black bartending vest, and my plastic name tag that proclaimed me "Ed"

At first, the usual boring drinks- white wine, gin and tonics ("not too much gin, Ed"), bloody Marys, club soda on the rocks.

Gonna be a long, sober evening at this rate.

I glanced around the room, trying to spot Gretchen. There she was, sitting on a couch with Eduardo. Her attention was riveted on him. Whatever he was saying held her spellbound. He was talking quietly, making occasional small hand gestures. I noticed several of his gestures included touching Gretchen on her leg, just below the hem of the short tight skirt she was wearing.

Eduardo said something to Gretchen as he stood up. He started toward my bar. Guess this genius will want orange juice on the rocks, I thought cynically.

Eduardo approached the bar. I was already reaching for the pitcher of orange juice. Skinny little fellow, I thought. Probably a vegetarian. My opinion of the whole witchcraft thing was in a power dive.

Eduardo put both hands on the bar, looked at my name tag and said softly, "Ed , make a Martini for the lady. Straight up. Olives. And make me a gin on the rocks, with water. Not too strong." He looked at me and smiled. Instantly, I had this guy nailed. A Martini straight up for Gretchen? Weak gin for him? This dude had a plan, I realized. He was gonna ply the Priestess with several Liquid Panty Removers while he nursed a weak gin and water. Several times, during the social hour, Eduardo was back, with the same order. As I mixed the fourth Martini, I looked past Eduardo over to the couch where Gretchen was sitting. Sure enough, ol' Eduardo's plan was working. Gretchen's skirt had ridden up; she had a slightly sloppy smile playing over her lips, and she was staring absently at Eduardo's back.

The Social hour ended. The High Priestess called for the Coven to gather around the podium. Eduardo was about to begin his pontificating.

As I packed up my utensils, I looked over to the Podium. Eduardo had donned reading glasses, and was looking at his notes. Gretchen was seated in the front row, idly playing with a strand of her black hair, focused as best as she could on Eduardo.

So, when the Gathering ended, there was a good chance that at least one witch would get naked, And Eduardo would continue his Mentoring. Hell, maybe he wasn't a vegetarian after all.

Try this one the next time someone wrinkles his nose at your liquor supply:

Abby and I were bartending for a ten year class reunion of a small upscale liberal arts college. Ten years out of school, and into new careers, these folks were anxious to impress one another- designer clothes, the mandatory BMW, and their TITLES, Vice President Jones, Doctor Smith, Senior Partner Shagnasty. Listening in on the bar chatter, nearly all these folks had second homes in Aspen, vacationed on St. Croix routinely, or had recently had cocktails with Mick Jagger. In other words, the bullshit was "knee high and risen' " Occasionally, Abby would look over to me with a grin and shake his head at some particularly questionable claim. Abby could spot a phony in a nanosecond
.

Early in the evening, a tall, tanned, and obviously Well Arrived thirty-something strode confidently up to the bar and stood tapping his recently manicured right hand on the bar, scanning the bottles. Bright yellow ascot offset a black silk shirt and matching jacket in black suede.

"Yours, Sir?" I asked, using a slightly differential tone in keeping with my lesser status among moguls.

"Well, I'd like a very dry Martini" (do I detect a slightly annoyed tone in his voice?) "but I insist on Boodles Gin. I can't stomach any of that bar swill you're pouring." He shook his stylishly shaggy razor cut slightly and said curtly, "Just give me a Heineken."

I sensed an opportunity to have a little fun.

"Well, my friend, I am forced to serve what your hosts have supplied me. But, as it happens, my partner always has a few choice brands set aside for the discriminating drinker, and I can just tell you're discriminating. Let me see what I can do."

Abby's trunk always contained a selection of upscale brands for use at the school when we had "live" classes and used real booze instead of colored water. Sure enough, he had a full bottle of Boodles. Who said there's no God?

I came back to the bar where Ascot was leaning casually, flashing a sparkling fortune of dental perfection at a slightly overweight blond in a low cut beige dress.He seemed as impressed with her cleavage as she was proud of it. He looked up as I approached the bar, and he flashed a smile at the sight of the bottle of Boodles.

"That's more like it," he said. "I'll have a very dry Martini, straight up. With a single olive."

"Coming right up, my good man" I replied. Then, after a pause, I said, "Not many people can tell the difference between makes of gin. It takes a trained and talented pallet to detect the difference. You obviously are a man of good taste and one who appreciates fine gin."

He snorted, and gave me a cocky smile. " I can tell the difference between Boodles and Tanguery blindfolded," he said with a smirk.. "And I wouldn't have that stuff (gesturing at the bar bottle of Seagrams) if I was stranded somewhere." He began tapping that manicured hand again, watching me make his Martini. His blond friend couldn't seem to take her eyes off him.

"Tell you what, sir" I said, "let's have a little fun before you try this Martini. I've never met anyone who can tell the difference in brands of gin. But, I have a feeling you are an exception to the rule. A connoisseur. Let me pour three shots of gin- one Boodles, the other two, bar brands. Impress your friend here with your discerning taste buds."

Ascot thought for a second, then grinned and winked at Cleavage. "Set 'em up," he said with a wink at the blond. He turned his back dramatically to the bar, so I could prepare the test. "This will be a piece a' cake," he said to the blond. I watched as he put his hand on her shoulder, then let it slip casually down her side until it stopped just under her right breast. I put three shot glasses on the bar; then took the Seagrams bottle from the bar and poured 3 equal shots of bar gin into each glass.

" Okay sir, all set." Ascot and the blond turned around to face me. Abby watched with obvious interest from the corner of the bar, his arms folded casually across his chest. He had listened to my conversation with Ascot.

"Three shots of gin, friend," I said. "Your challenge is to identify the Boodles."

Ascot went to work, picking up each shot glass; sniffing it, swirling it, holding it up to the light. Taking small tastes, casting his eyes Heavenward, he attempted to identify the unique (at least in his mind) taste of the Boodles.

Finally, after several minutes of sniffing, peering, and swirling, he pushed one shot glass toward me roughly."Well, I'm having a little trouble with these two here," he said pointing to the two glasses closest to him. "One is

Tanquery, I'm sure. The other is Boodles. But the stuff in that glass is the worst excuse for gin I've ever tasted."

I looked Ascot in the eye, smiled and said, "They're all Seagrams, pal….all three of 'em from that bottle right there."

Ascot looked at the three shot glasses. He glanced over at Abby, who flashed him a bright smile. His face reddening and without a word to Cleavage, he picked up his Martini and walked away from the bar. The blond looked first at me, then at Abby; shook her head slightly with a smile, and joined a group of her friends.

I looked over to where Abby was leaning against the bar, the smile still on his face. He gave me thumbs up, then turned to serve a customer.

"Man," I thought to myself; "what a great gig!"

Chapter 7

Crap...Fifteen More To Go

If I had invented the game of golf, it would have been the front seven and the back seven. Certainly not eighteen holes. And any stroke within fifty yards of the hole would only count for half. Why in blazes should a stinking putt of thirteen inches count the same as a drive of two hundred yards? Those crazy Scots.

After fourteen holes of golf, I'm tired, sweaty, discouraged and generally in a rotten mood. Every bit of my DNA is focused on how much longer this misery can possibly last. Hmm, four more holes times fifteen minutes per hole....another hour ...one more hour out of my life, hacking at that stupid ball.

So why do I play golf? It's hardly a choice in the business world. Tell a client or associate that you don't play golf and you're immediately branded as being hopelessly out of place, especially if you have anything to do with sales or marketing. So, ever since entering the world of business, I've been a golfer. Well, I've played at being a golfer.

The memory of my first golf game after accepting the job of Sales Engineer for a Midwest manufacturer is sharply etched into my brain. A tournament, organized by the guys in the sales department. To be played at the brand new Pete Dye course just outside of town.

"You bet, sign me up," I told Dick, the organizer of the tournament. I didn't own a set of clubs, or golf shoes, or balls, but everybody else in the department was playing, including the Boss. To not play would have been unthinkable.

I overheard one of the other new guys in the department talking about the new set of clubs he'd bought. So as we went through the cafeteria line at lunch, I asked him if he'd traded his old set in. "Nope," replied Ron. "They wouldn't take 'em. Said they'd never be able to sell 'em. Why?"

I told him I'd like to play in the department tournament, but didn't have any clubs. As he reached for a piece of cherry pie to go with his cheeseburger and fries, he said, "I'll make you a hell of a deal on those clubs. Two woods, five irons, and a bag- I'll let you have the whole set for thirty dollars. And, I'll throw in the balls that are in the bag."

I told him I'd let him know tomorrow. After all, we were on a tight budget; school loans, the car payment, baby food. I'd have to check with my wife.

She was all for it when I tentatively brought up the subject at supper. "You need to play golf if you are going to get ahead in business. And, you'll be able to play with Daddy when he visits."

Her Dad was a passionate golfer. Played any chance he could. He was a natural athlete, and was proud of his game. He'd been after me to take up the game for several years.

So I called Ron and told him he had a deal, that I'd have the check the next day. He agreed to bring the clubs to work.

The next day at lunch, we went out to his car. He opened the trunk and pulled out a faded red canvas bag with a brown leather strap. The clubs were probably twenty years old, he said. "Bought 'em used when I was in college. They're a little scuffed, but I've hit some damned fine shots with those. They'll do you a good job." I gave him my check.

I'd played softball and baseball in school and had found it natural to swing left handed, even though I'm right-handed in everything else I do. Later that evening, after supper, I took my new clubs out to the back yard, behind the wretchedly hot apartments we lived in, along with other new

116

hires at the Company. I took the driver out, and discovered it was a right-handed club.

Rats. I hadn't even thought of that little detail. Shoulda asked. But, I thought, let's give her a try. I assumed what I thought to be a proper golf stance and swung the club right handed. Holy Smoke, I thought. That's the most unnatural thing I've ever tried. How could anyone on the planet ever swing right- handed? I tried several more times, that sinking feeling getting worse with each swing.

My friend John came out of his apartment, carrying a cup of coffee. It was still about 90 degrees. John was in baggy plaid Bermuda shorts, a white tee shirt and was bare footed. His two- year old daughter, clad in a diaper, followed him, one tiny hand hanging onto the leg of his Bermudas.

"New set of clubs, eh?" John was from Wisconsin, and had that clipped way of talking.

"Yeah, new to me, anyway. Bought 'em today. Trouble is, I really think I need left- handed clubs. Swinging right handed just isn't natural."

John grinned, sat his coffee cup down on the concrete slab that was our back stoop, and popped a pacifier in his daughter's mouth. He took the driver from me, looked at it and said, "There's no such thing as a good left-handed golfer. Golf was intended to be played right- handed. Forget that left- handed stuff. Just watch me."

He took the stance. Paused. Brought the club back smoothly and swung viciously. "Not bad," he said examining the club head, his thinning blond hair matted to his forehead in the clinging humidity. "These clubs have some great shots left in 'em. You playing in the sales tournament?" I told him I was. "But John," I said, "I don't have any golf shoes. Are tennis shoes okay?"

John retrieved his coffee cup and his little daughter, who was concentrating on her pacifier. He turned to me with a grin and said, "They call 'em tennis shoes for a reason. You really need a set of golf cleats to anchor your stance."

He swung his little daughter up and around to straddle his neck and started toward his apartment. "See you tomorrow," he said in that Wisconsin twang. Anchor my stance? What, I was gonna be in danger of sliding off the golf course? Here I was, a lefty with a set of right- handed clubs. It was Wednesday. I had two days to master a right-handed golf swing. It was 4 days until payday, and now I needed golf shoes so as not to be branded a complete nincompoop. What a stupid situation to be in.

And they call golf a game? My stomach was already starting to knot up.

Saturday. Tournament day.

The Sales Department Outing started at 11:00 am. I left our apartment at around 9, hoping to get some time on the driving range. I hadn't yet mastered the right- handed swing, And I didn't have golf cleats. Maybe no one would notice I was wearing my U.S. Keds.

I packed my red canvas bag with nine clubs in the back seat of our '59 Renault Dauphine and headed out to the golf course. Maybe I'll get in a traffic accident and won't be able to make it in time to play, I thought to myself. Or maybe it'll rain.

A quick glance at the cloudless sky was stark assurance that rain was nowhere in sight. Crap. I was gonna have to play. I pulled into the parking lot, found a space for the Renault and got out. All around me, the other sales department guys were unloading their clubs and changing into their golf shoes. The knot in my stomach tightened. These guys looked like they couldn't wait to get on the golf course.

There was Bill, who had the Steelcase desk right in front of me at the office. He was leaning against his Buick, lacing up his saddle patterned golf shoes. A professional looking leather bag of clubs was propped against his car. Over there, my friend John, already outfitted in his black golf shoes (no socks), his full set of clubs attesting to his ability.

I took my little red canvas golf bag out of the car and walked over to where Bill was tying the knot in his shoe. I hoped against hope he wouldn't mention my black U.S. Keds.

"Looks like a great day for golf, Bill," I said trying to sound confident and cheerful, but feeling nothing but dread. Why couldn't it rain?

Bill looked me up and down. He had on crisp black Bermudas, with a white golf shirt, and a lightweight, sleeveless pullover. I had chosen my favorite cutoffs, a light green t-shirt, and white wool socks under my Keds. I thought I detected a slight smirk as he reached for his golf bag.

"Any day on the golf course is a good day," he said. "By the way, what's your handicap?"

Handicap? I could think of any number of handicaps. Never having played a round of golf was probably a handicap. Right- handed clubs and a left-handed swing probably qualified. How about a case of nerves that had me on the verge of throwing up? Was that a handicap?

But I said, "Bill I actually don't think I have an official handicap." "I assumed as much," Bill said casually. "Maybe you'll get with some other guys who are just starting out, and you can get some practice." I relaxed a little. Surely there were some other guys who were just starting out, and I could play with them.

When we got to the clubhouse, I looked at the Official Pairings. I was in a foursome with Bill, John, and my Boss. My stomach knotted. I felt the panic build. Please God, just strike me dead here. Why allow me to suffer through five hours of certain agony?

No such luck. No lightning bolts. No comets streaking down from the heavens to take me out of my misery. I walked over to where the carts were parked, arranged in the order we were to tee off. I tried to blend in with the crowd of boisterous, laughing golfers, all of whom seemed anxious to get started. I, on the other hand, kept hoping for an attack of appendicitis or maybe an earthquake to put this off till another day- or forever.

I found my foursome. Bill in his spiffy togs talking to Fred, my boss, as he loaded his clubs onto Fred's cart. Good old Bill never missed an opportunity to suck up to management. Fred was attired in black slacks, a white golf shirt, and a stylish sleeveless black sweater, his black golf shoes gleaming.

I put my red canvas bag of clubs on the cart next to John's, and took a minute to look at John's arsenal: Four woods, in knitted University of Wisconsin socks with tassels; a full set of irons; a water ball retriever and an umbrella. Brushes and towels hung from loops on the bag. All he was missing was an M-1 in case we encountered the Viet Cong in the sand traps. John was on the practice green, concentrating on putt after putt.

Maybe that's what I need, I thought to myself. Maybe a little practice would relieve the ….. Ah, shit! I didn't have any golf balls! In my worry over having to play, I had completely forgotten to get to K-Mart for golf balls and tees.

I hollered over to John, "I'll be right back. Gotta run up to the clubhouse for a sec!" As I turned, I could see John scowl at me for missing a putt. Loosen up John, I thought. It's just a game.

Four dollars and fifty cents for three balls? (It was 1967, remember.) Good night. I'd have to take my lunch from home all next week. Better get at least six, I thought. I'd heard there were some water holes on the course, and they kept talking about the high rough. With a little bag of tees, I left the clubhouse, just over ten dollars lighter in the pocket.

I got back to the carts where John, Fred and Bill were laughing about something. I took some comfort from John's attire. Like me, John looked like he was ready for yard work. John was a big man; about six- four, and his college football muscle was turning beefy. He had on wrinkled khaki shorts, a white tee shirt, but at least he had real golf shoes with cleats. I could feel my face redden as Fred glanced down at my U.S. Keds.

"I didn't know you were a golfer, Ed," said Fred, with a smile.

"Well, I haven't played much," I replied, trying to match his easy banter. "Just got my first set of clubs. John gave me a tip or two." From the corner of my eye, I could see a look of surprise cross John's face, but he didn't say anything.

The announcement came from the clubhouse, over the loudspeaker. The tournament was about to start. There were six- foursomes, and we'd all tee off on the number one hole. It was suddenly and starkly clear to me that mine was the first foursome. That meant we'd tee off with every member of the sales department watching. Twenty- three sets of eyes were on me as I hit my first ever tee shot. My stomach knotted. My legs turned to jelly, and I suddenly felt I had to have a bowel movement. But it was too late.

"Fred's group on the tee box please," came the metallic sounding announcement from the clubhouse. Fred walked confidently up to the marker, stooped to place his ball on the tee, and straightened up.

He's wearing a glove, I thought to myself. Just one glove. I glanced around. All the guys had a glove on their left hand. Guess I really should have read up on golf before now, I thought.

Fred took his stance and smoothly drove his shot straight down the fairway, a beautiful golf shot. "Ah, crap!" said Fred as he watched his ball roll to a stop. "I pulled it." He picked up his tee and walked toward us, clearly unhappy about his shot.

Man, I thought, if I could hit a shot like that, I'd commit my life to the Lord, give up swearing, and go to Church every Sunday. If Fred was unhappy with it, I wondered what a good shot looked like?

Bill was next. He looked the part of a seasoned and well-decked out professional. He casually teed up and stepped back to line up his shot. One practice swing, and then he drilled his ball past Fred's. The waiting golfers roared their approval. "Great shot Bill, close to three hundred yards."

John looked at me questioningly, but I nodded for him to go ahead. My knees were shaking so hard that I had to lean against the bench for support. My bowels were bubbling. Had to be nerves, I thought. Maybe there was a toilet at the first green.

John sauntered up to the tee, his linebacker confidence showing in his swagger and the look of determination on his face. He jammed his ball and tee into the ground, straightened and took a full and ferocious practice swing. He hollered over to Bill, "Watch this Alice." Then he blasted his shot a full 40 yards beyond Bill's. He grinned broadly as Fred and the other guys whistled and slapped his shoulders.

Fred turned to me. "Okay, Eddie, lets get another one out there."

Please, God, just let me hit it straight and at least to the fairway.

I pushed away from the bench and walked haltingly to the tee. Was that my appendix about to let go? No, I decided, just my bowels cramping.

I tried to put my tee in the ground. My hand was shaking so badly I couldn't get the ball to stay on the tee. I got down on one knee and, using both hands, finally got it teed up. I straightened up. The crowd was still. I could feel every eye on me, on my U.S. Keds, on my cutoffs, on my gloveless hand. I took what I thought was the stance and took a practice swing.

My club hit the ground hard, sending shock waves up my arms and across my shoulders, hard enough to rock the ball off the tee with the vibration. I heard some of the guys chuckle.

"Go ahead, Eddie, we won't count that one," Fred said.

I got the ball back on the tee. I decided against a practice swing. Instead, I pulled the club back and swung with everything I had...and this time missed the ball completely. It sat there on the tee, undisturbed. Some of the guys turned to hide their grins and stifle their laughter.

Now I was a complete wreck. Two attempts in front of my friends, my boss. I had to hit that ball. Almost blindly, I swung again. This time I felt contact. I opened my eyes, looked down the fairway to find my ball. "Hey, Ed," one of the guys in the back yelled, "you almost made it to the women's tee." Even Fred joined in the laughter. I walked down the tee box to where my ball had stopped and started to hit it again.

"Tee off from the white tees!" ordered the metallic voice over the loudspeaker.

"That's his *fourth* shot!" yelled back one of the guys in the crowd. That did it. The group now roared with laughter. I tried to laugh with them, but inside, I wanted to disappear in a blast of fire and smoke, like the witch in Oz.

Mercifully, I hit the ball with the next attempt, and it made it to the fringe of the fairway. "That one's in play, Eddie," Fred said in encouragement.

Wonderful. Only seventeen more holes to go.

Some people must be born with a bunch of athletic genes that are absolutely absent in my DNA. I have never mastered the game of golf, in spite of hacking around for almost 40 years. And, unlike those happy Callaway-armed fanatics who drool over the prospect of a 7:00 AM tee time every Saturday, I don't enjoy it. But, if you are a fast-talking, back slapping sales guy, you gotta play golf, right? At least, that's what I'd always thought.

My father-in-law, Houston, was an avid golfer. Played twice a week, and entered every tournament he came across. He was a natural athlete, a great basketball player in his day, a deadly slam shot on the ping- pong table, and nearly a scratch golfer. So, anytime we'd visit the in-laws, I was obligated to play in his foursome. We played at his course built into the rolling hills of West Virginia. The course had been built on land that had been a farm. And the course designer had left a barn on the edge of the third fairway, a big barn, the old fashioned kind with a haymow on the upper floor and a big window on both ends of the mow.

The first time I played that course with Houston, that barn gave Houston yet another excuse to critique my attempt at golf. Houston's tee shot was a beauty, landing in the fairway just beyond the edge of the barn. I, on the other hand, was just short of the barn after two dreadful, but by now standard, shots from the tee. The fairway broke left beyond the barn to the green, a five iron away from where Houston's ball had come to rest. From where my ball was, the barn was directly between me and the green.

"What's the best way for me to approach the green?" I called out to Houston. He was waiting impatiently for me to pull up my socks and play golf.

"Hell," he responded, "from where you are the shortest way is to go through the hay mow."

He was kidding. I took him seriously.

I looked at the opening to the haymow, about fifty feet away and fifteen feet up. I could see the opening on the far end of the barn. Must be how all the locals do it, I thought.

For the first time that day, my club connected perfectly. The ball soared straight for the barn, following that satisfying "click" that announces a well hit ball. My ball slammed into the front of the barn and bounced straight back at me, missing me by several feet and rolling almost all the way back to the tee box. The foursome waiting to tee off just stared at the ball, then me, shaking their heads. "What in blazes are you doing?" hollered Houston, driving up in his cart. "You aimed right at the barn!" He was shaking his head in disgust.

"You told me to go through the haymow," I replied. My face reddened as I heard the guys on the tee laughing at my stupidity.

Houston kept shaking his head, "If I told you to wipe your rear end with a broken bottle, would you do it?"

I walked back to get my ball thinking golf was perhaps the most over-rated, stupid game on the planet.

Golf intimidates me. Rather, I allow myself to be intimidated by it. But with my experience so far, I have good reason to be intimidated. I am truly capable of making a complete and total ass of myself on the golf course.

I'm King of the Driving Range! Get me get out on the range with a bucket of balls, and no pressure, and I can hit the ball a mile. Straight, like Tiger. Chip, like Arnold Palmer.

But, get me on the first tee, with three pairs of eyes watching my every move, and I get as uptight as a first timer facing a proctology exam. I freeze up like the Tin Man in a driving rainstorm. Especially in one of those dreaded business scrambles where you are likely to get paired with three complete strangers. And with my luck, they are strangers who probably live to play golf.

I have enjoyed playing from time to time, believe it or not. When I first started playing golf, I played Saturdays with my pal Jack, and two other good ol' boys whose names are long since forgotten. We'd get to a small public course in southern Indiana around 9:00, play golf, drink beer, and to hell with keeping score. My kinda golf! Why can't it be like that all the time?

Then there are my pals Don, Truman, and Jim. Good golfers. Take the game seriously, every one of them. They all shoot in the 80's. Practice all the time. But I enjoy playing with them. They have patience, and encourage me. If I hit a duffer shot (If? How about every other shot?), they just casually say, "Slow down your swing next time," or something else helpful like that. Those guy's are a rarity in golf, guys who just enjoy being on the course.

If only the world was full of Dons, Trumans, or Jims.

Golf is full of anal-retentive types. I played with a business associate a few years back, a guy I needed to get to know better. We played at his club on a cold, blustery day. (As much as I hated to play golf anyway, I REALLY hate to play in the cold.)

At the end of the first hole, Joe, who was keeping score, asked me what I had.

"I think I have a seven," I answered, honestly. (Who could keep track of all these swings?)

"No, Ed, you had an eight." Then Joe proceeded to tick off every shot I'd hit on that first hole. Jeez….

The next hole was a par three over a small lake. Joe laid up on the green, within five feet of the cup.

My shot dropped unceremoniously in the middle of the lake. A typical Ed Friel shot. Guess Joe will want to count that one just like in real golf. Damn, I hate this stupid game.

Chapter 8

It's the Union, Jack!

"God in Heaven, what happened to that concrete stanchion?" The foreman acted like he couldn't believe his eyes.

"You told us to take it down, to level it with the floor," I replied. My stomach tightened with fear. Had we misunderstood the foreman? Had we made some horrible mistake? Would my friend Johnny and I get fired the first day of our summer job at the mill?

Every summer, the paper mill in Chillicothe hired about thirty college kids to cover vacations taken by employees. We were called the Extra Crew, and were assigned to low-level manual jobs all over the mill. When a regular took vacation, the rest of the full time crew would move around to fill in on the various job positions, and then an Extra Crewman would take up the lowest level job to round out the crew. It was dirty, hot work, but it paid well. Most summer days, the mill would be short handed, and an extra crewman could work double shifts of 16 hours straight to earn more money. In the early '60's, a summer's worth of work in the mill could almost pay for a full year of college.

I was hired the year I graduated from Chillicothe High,. My Old Man knew a foreman and he put in a good word. I took the job with mixed feelings. I was working my dream job on WCHI radio, as a disc jockey and newscaster. I worked all the hours I could at the radio station, but that job didn't pay well enough to build up the old college fund. So I started at the mill. Many days, I'd work the morning shift on the air, then head to the mill for the second shift. Working the 3:00 PM to 11:00 PM. shift as a sweat and grime covered grunt brought me back to reality.

On that first morning on the job, Johnny and I were assigned to a maintenance crew. The foreman took us deep into the basement of one of the machine buildings. He told us a new paper machine was to be installed there and that our job was to do some preparation work before

129

construction began. He walked us over to a corner of the basement, to a huge block of concrete, probably six feet square and four feet high.

"This was one of the original supports for the old machine," the foreman told us. " I want you guys to take that jackhammer and knock it down. Make it level with the floor. Haul the pieces out and pile 'em over there. We'll get the debris with a loader."

He showed us how to use the big jackhammer, and left us on our own. "I'll be back in a couple a hours," he called out over his shoulder as he walked up the circular steel ladder that went up to the main machine room.

Johnny and I decided we'd better get our eighteen-year-old butts in gear to make a good impression on our new boss. At about 7:20, I went to work with the jackhammer. It took some getting used to, but eventually the chips were flying. Johnny and I took turns riding the hammer, and shoveling the chunks into a wheelbarrow. By 10:00, we had the block broken into small chunks and hauled outside, and piled for the loader. Then we used the hammer to make the floor as smooth as our inexperience would let us. That's when the foreman came back.

"But where in hell is the block? That thing was huge. That should have taken you guys a couple of days." He took off his "Pulp, Sulfite and Paper Mill Workers" branded cap and wiped the sweat from the top of his balding head.

"Sir," Johnny said hesitantly, "that hammer is a righteous tool. There's nothing to that job with the right tools. Besides, we're new. We didn't want you to think we were just a couple of goof offs. We need the job."

I nodded in anxious agreement. The foreman stood there for a few moments, staring at the smooth place in the floor where the block once stood. Dust hung in the air. There was a steady hum from the big paper machines on the floor above. Finally the foreman turned to us. "Boys, you're gonna make the rest of us look bad if you work like this all summer."

He cleared his throat and hawked a glob of phlegm onto the floor.

"We're union," he said. "This is our job. We're here all the time. You guys are just here for the summer. You got to slow down. We'd a stretched this here job out for a day. Maybe two, what with breaks, the hammer needin' repairs. That kinda thing. Now, you guys get brooms and kind a sweep up in here. Take breaks. Maybe re-pile that concrete. Look busy. But just stretch this job out at least 'til quittin' time." He put his hat back on and turned to go back up the spiral stairs.

Johnny and I just looked at one another. We both shrugged and said, almost in unison, "We're Union," and went off in search of brooms.

I'm sure unions had their place at one time. At least, that's what I've heard. My own limited experience with unions just re-affirms my first impression at the mill that unions are the adult equivalent of day care.

I got my orders one Monday to report to Dock 3. That was the railroad dock near the center of the mill, where boxcars containing bags and barrels of starch and chemicals were unloaded. Six of us were assigned to unload a boxcar of fifty-five gallon drums of chemicals. I was the extra crewmember.

I got a wheel cart and started taking the barrels into the warehouse,. After about twenty minutes, one of the old-timers stopped me as I re-entered the boxcar to get another drum.

"Slow down, boy," he said, gripping my arm. "We got all day. You don't want to be in any hurry to get this done. The Union's got a standard time to unload a car like this. Don't be makin' us look bad. Let's take us a break". So we did. The entire crew took a sit-down break, after less than half an hour on the job. I stood there fidgeting, anxious to get back to work. I didn't want to be branded as lazy by the boss.

Hell, not much chance of that, I discovered. At that moment, I spotted the foreman, sitting on the dock, leaning up against the wall, cigarette dangling, his eyes closed in blissful, unconcerned relaxation.

Right then and there I saw these guys didn't need any outside help to make themselves look bad. Little wonder unions are called, "the working man's friend."

One morning I was the extra man on #2 Coater. It is a block long, state of the art machine that applied a special high gloss coating to the big rolls of paper. Later, they were cut into packages of office bond paper. The uncoated rolls, nearly eight feet wide, and weighing nearly a ton, were suspended on the front of the machine. The paper passed through a coating spray at high speed and then through gas fired ovens where it dried. The coated paper was then wound onto a new roll. It took about twenty minutes to run each roll through the entire process. The finished rolls were placed on heavy wood steel-wheeled wagons as they came off the coater. It was my job to pull those wagons, by hand to an elevator; take it down one level, and to manhandle the huge roll onto a storage bench.

The control center for #2 Coater was up a flight of steel stairs near the front of the machine. It was an instrument filled room where the Machine Tender held court. He monitored the workings of the coater from a steel desk and office chair. He was "the Man in Charge." The Machine Tender was like the captain of a ship. I was returning from the basement with my wagon, after wrestling yet another roll onto the bench. It seemed like the run would never end. As I trudged across the floor, I heard a voice from above. I looked up. It was Shorty, the Machine Tender on that shift. He motioned me to come up.

I put my wagon in its place near the Coater and started up the stairs. Shorty beckoned me again, with an urgent look on his face. But it was far too noisy in the cavernous coating room to hear him talk unless you were face to face.

I approached Shorty at the top of the stairs. He was just over five feet tall, with a huge soft belly that made him appear even shorter. His Oshkosh coveralls were rolled up at the cuff, exposing white wool socks and steel-toed work boots. His white tee shirt was sweat stained and smudged. A "Pulp, Sulfite and Paper Mill Workers" cap was pulled down to his ears. He stared at me through thick safety glasses.

"Boy," he shouted over the din of the machine, "run down and tell the foreman to get hisself up here. I got to take me a shit." He pointed to toward the restroom down on the main floor, then motioned me to hurry up and get moving.

I went down the stairs and spotted the foreman midway down the length of the coater. He was talking to a young man in a sport shirt, carrying a clipboard. I walked up to the foreman, and waited until he turned to me. Out of the corner of my eye, I spotted Shorty high above, leaning on the stair railing, watching me intently.

"Shorty said to tell you to come up and watch the machine for a few minutes," I said. "He's got to take a shit."

The foreman frowned at me. He winked at the young engineer and told me, "Son, go back up there and tell Shorty he ain't got time to take a shit." I had my orders, I guessed. He was the Foreman. I was just the Extra Crew. I turned and walked the length of the floor, and back up the stairs. I walked up close to Shorty and shouted, "The boss says you ain't got time to take a shit."

Shorty's eyes snapped. His jaw dropped as if he'd been slapped. He stared at me for just a moment, then shouted loud enough for me and the foreman to hear, "A man ain't got much of a job if he ain't got time to take a shit!"

He turned, went into the control cab and hit the big red 'Stop' button. The huge machine began to wind down. The strand of paper in the oven broke and flamed up inside the fireproof enclosure. Shorty stormed out the back to the door of the cab. He shot me a look of contempt as he marched down the stairs toward the men's locker room.

The foreman beckoned me down to the floor. "Looks like you got your work cut out for you, son. When that oven cools down, get in there and get that mess cleaned up. We got an order to run."

I'd heard that old saying, "shit rolls downhill." Now I saw how it played out in real life. When Shorty took his contentedly in the men's room, the Boss just rolled it down to me, gift-wrapped. I crawled into that hot oven to clean it out as Shorty emerged from the john looking like he felt one hundred percent better. He and the foreman probably had a good laugh over "that smart ass college kid humpin' and sweatin' it out.

Fine with me, I fumed to myself. In another three months or so, I'd be back in class at Ohio State checking out those hot college babes. You chumps will still be here, doin' shift work, where you "ain't got time to take a shit."

Shift work was a new experience. At the mill, all the regular workers rotated weekly to a different shift. Same mind-numbing job performed on a different schedule. They'd work a week on first shift. Then on Sunday, they would work first shift, 7:00 AM-3:00 PM, then "double back" to start the new week on third shift, 11:00 PM-7:00 AM. And so forth, 52 weeks a year.

Extra Crew worked shifts that needed a body. Many times, at the end of an eight-hour shift, the foreman would ask, "They need a man over on cutters. You wanna work another eight?"

But it wasn't really a question. You turned the opportunity down at your own risk. And it did offer one benefit. Pay for the second eight-hour shift was at 'time and a half.' We were young, full of piss and vinegar. Who the heck needed to sleep eight hours every night?

The first night I pulled 16 hours straight was also the first time I'd ever had minestrone soup. I went in at 3:00 in the afternoon. It was second shift at the mill. I'd already done five hours on the air at WCHI from 9:00 AM until 2:00 PM. Then I hot-footed it over to the mill for 8 hours of stuffing reams of paper into boxes. Around 10:00pm, the foreman asked me if I could do another shift. "Your replacement called in sick," he said.

Crap. Eight more hours doing this. But, at time and a half, right? Right.

Around 2:30 AM, the lunch wagon came through our department. I was dead on my feet. It was all I could do to stay awake. I'd actually dozed off on my feet at the end of the cutter line, and was jolted awake by reams of paper hitting my feet. I thought maybe some food or coffee would revive me. Or maybe some soup. Mom was pretty good in the soup department- beef vegetable, great chili. But I'd never heard of minestrone soup. I bought a bowl, along with a salami sandwich. And black coffee. I ate it all in the thirty minutes allotted for "lunch".

3:45 AM. I was still struggling to stay awake, to keep up with the endless flow of paper, with "20 Weight Bond" printed importantly over the green packaging paper that wrapped it.

That's when my bowels announced themselves.

Suddenly I was wide-awake. The initial stomach cramps seemed to keep time with the flow of paper. Each time I stuffed exactly twelve reams in a box, folded the top just so, and sent it through the sealing machine, I got that all too familiar cramping.

The Line Chief, at the front of the cutter, controlled the flow of work. The flow of my bowels, on the other hand, seemed under the control of the Devil. I had to get to the bathroom. I could sense an imminent disaster. I was about to lose control of the old sphincter muscle. I had a bad taste in my mouth. What was it? Wait a minute. Ah no. That stupid soup. Minestrone. And spicy salami. And coffee.

I was alone at the end of the cutter line. The noise of the machines drowned out any attempt to shout for help. No one was close enough to signal. I contemplated filling my pants for the first time since diapers. And I hadn't brought a change of clothes.

Suddenly, I had no other choice. To hell with the 20 Weight Bond. I bolted for the men's room. An empty stall. Pants down. Blessed Relief. Barely in the nick of time

Afterwards, I hurried back to my post. "What in hell do you think you're doin' asshole?" the foreman asked, , "leavin' the job in the middle of a run?" Red faced, he leaned into my face. Reams of paper littered the floor where I was supposed to be putting them in boxes.

"Sir," I said quickly. "I usually have a cast iron stomach, but whatever was in that miserable soup on the roach wagon backfired on me. I had a case of the shits I could write an opera about." Go ahead, I thought to myself; fire me. I could care. I really could. I'm miserable. Dead tired. My stomach was still cramping. I wanted go crawl off to bed for about a week.

The foreman stared at me, his eyes catching glints of hard factory lighting. Then a slight smile crossed his lips.

"Guess there's no real harm done. Clean up this mess. Then get you some Alka Seltzer. You still got three more hours to go."

I thought, maybe these Union guys aren't so bad after all.

Several weeks later, I got to the mill for second shift. My foreman said "Son, they want you to work over in the coaters today. They got a big order and it's gonna take most of the night. You'll probably get stuck workin' third trick too."

Great! It was the middle of the afternoon, and I was being sent to my least favorite department. Extra Crew working in the Coating department almost never worked just 8 hours. It was routine to get stuck for 2 shifts.

And the work was heavy. We helped the Third Hand on take a finished roll of paper off the coating machine. Then we helped lower a hollow steel tube, eight feet long and a foot in diameter in place with a crane to receive more paper. The machine never stopped.

Sometimes, the paper failed to take to the new core and paper spilled out onto the floor. Guess who got to collect all that paper and put it in a wheeled bin? Then guess who got to push that heavy bin to the recycling room.

The main part of my job was to help lower the big roll of paper onto a heavy steel wheeled wood wagon, and then take it down one floor and push the roll onto a wooden bench. You pulled the wagon by hand to the elevators, and pushed the roll onto the bench. Each roll weighed 1800 to 2000 pounds. By the time I got back upstairs, another roll was ready to come off. There was no such thing as a break, unless the endless strand of paper broke. But that just meant more work for me, picking up all that paper.

That afternoon, I trudged through the mill to the coating department, cursing my luck. I couldn't wait for school to start so I could get some rest and away from those stupid coaters.

As I started into the coater room, I saw a small crowd of people gathered around the stairwell that went down one level to the shipping room. The stairwell was next to the big freight elevators. There was a big forklift with a crane parked beside the stairwell. Curious, I walked closer.

"Good Lord! What the heck happened?" I asked one of the guys. A huge roll of paper was lodged in the stairwell. One of the wood wagons was crushed under it. He shook his head. He was one of the full timers. A heavyset man, in bib overalls and white tee shirt. I knew he worked as Backtender on the #2 coater.

"You know that new extra man we got? The big guy. Wears glasses and looks kinda stupid?" He grinned, showing bad teeth. A small dribble of Mail Pouch inched down from the corner of his mouth. He wiped it with the back of his hand.

"We told him to take that wagon with the roll of paper downstairs, and push it off onto the bench. And that's exactly what he did. Or tried to, anyway. Never dawned on us we'd have to tell him to take the elevator. Hell, he's a college man. Supposed to be smart." He continued to shake his head and chuckle. "What a dumb-ass."

"You mean he tried to take that load down those STAIRS?" I asked incredulously, looking down staircase. It was probably six feet wide with steel steps, a landing halfway down , and then a 180 degree turn, to continue to the floor below. "Is the guy dead?" "Naw, he's okay. Scared shitless though, I'll tell you that. He pulled that wagon down the first coupla stairs. Then the paper roll started to slide. Lucky for him it wedged before it pinned him to the wall. He'd be deader'n four o'clock. Busted the wheels right off that wagon!"

It took most of the second shift to lift that roll of paper out of the stairwell, but that was left to the maintenance department. It didn't stop the action in the coating department. I finally got out of there around 5:00 AM. Fourteen hours pulling those stupid rolls, but at least I had the common sense to use the elevator.

Chapter 9

Ain't No Such Thing as a Bald Headed Rock Star

Brother John

One of my many fantasies in life was to be a rock star (as recounted in Chapter 4). And, as you know, the key reason I had no hope whatsoever of being a rock star is a breathtaking lack of any discernable talent for the guitar…or for singing. The only thing I had going for me was a full head of black hair, and as one long forgotten girlfriend told me when I was a junior in high school, a faint and distant resemblance to Ricky Nelson.

Even that started to go wrong during my freshman year in college. I began to find a few black hairs in the tub after washing my hair. I wondered if… Certainly not me! Couldn't be! I had a widow's peak, just like Ricky and Elvis…. I was destined to be a rock star or a network newsman. Hair was a prerequisite. I simply couldn't be losing my hair.

My grandfather (on my mother's side) was bald. As were all my uncles on mom's side of the family. Cue ball bald. With just that little horseshoe fringe around the sides. I'd read somewhere, probably in Reader's Digest, that baldness is hereditary. If your relatives on your mother's side of the family are bald, chances are fabulous that you will, indeed, be just as bald as they are. The good news, you'll save money on haircuts.

One summer evening, after a long day at my summer job at the paper mill, I'd taken a shower, washed my hair, and was watching TV. Mom came into the living room and said, "There are a lot of black hairs in the tub. Do you think you're starting to lose your hair? My Dad started to lose his hair when he was about your age. I'll bet you wind up looking just like Papa."

She actually sounded cheerful!

My stomach tightened. Even Mom had noticed the hair in the tub! Crap…it can't be true! I can't be losing my hair! I went into the bathroom and looked carefully into the mirror. Nope. I looked just the same. No visible sign of a bald spot. The widow's peak was still there.

False alarm, I thought. But…the hair in the shower was black. Who had showered before me? Dad? No, he took a shower in the basement. My brother John? His hair was brown. Mom? My grandmother? Crap…the evidence was irrefutable. The long black hairs were mine! Aargh!!!

I started paying attention to all the great rock stars; Mick and Keith, Bill and Charlie of the Stones; Paul, Ringo, and George. They all had their hair, and showed no sign of losing it. What the heck was their secret? These guys decided to make a career of rock 'n roll, and their hair stayed in. I, on the other hand, was destined to be a rock star. And now this?

The only rock singer I knew facing baldness was Mike Love of the Beach Boys. He had taken to wearing a cap, and growing a beard- a dead giveaway that he had SOMETHING TO HIDE. Ol' Mike was no dummy. All the other Beach Boys had proper heads of Rock Star Hair. He knew if he was to have an equal shot at all those groupies, he was going to have to hide the fact that he was BALD.

Wonder if he wore that hat to bed? Rats. Talk about a funk.

I started to pay attention to all the anchors and reporters on the TV news. I decided if the music business didn't work out long term, if I only had a few hit records, and had to do something else, I'd be an anchorman on TV news. After all, I had established myself as one of the stars of Chillicothe radio. So it was natural that I could transfer that talent to television.

My funk deepened as I studied all the network anchors. Huntley, Brinkley, Cronkite. All had hair. So did the reporters. Hell, even the local news guys on Columbus, Ohio TV had hair. Not a bald guy in sight. WHY ME? Why not John, my brother? He wasn't interested in being a rock star, or a TV personality. In fact, based on John's favorite thing to do, he was probably hoping to be a Professional TV Watcher. He was addicted to the Little Rascals and Laurel and Hardy.

The Old Man practically had to drag him outside on weekends to get him away from the Saturday cartoons.

But as John got older, his hair was full and intact. What rotten luck. He was blessed with the head of hair that I needed!

By the third year of college (Ohio State College of Commerce) it was apparent the hair loss was real. Even though I still wore my hair long and styled like Elvis and Ricky, you could see daylight through the top of my coiffure. One day, as we were walking across campus, my roommate said, "Ed you're losing your hair. I can see right through it. You're gonna be bald as an egg in a few years!"

Bill was going to be an engineer. Wore a slide rule on his belt. His pocket protector bristled with pencils and pens. He had a flattop, shaved close on the sides. Oh, a full head of hair, all right. He just didn't appreciate it. Got it cut every two weeks.

Bill liked Sinatra and the big bands. He thought Elvis was a no talent hillbilly, and that Ricky was just lucky to be born into show business. "Why don't you get a decent haircut?" he'd say. "What makes you think you look like Elvis? At least, Elvis doesn't have zits."

Thanks for really making me crazy, Bill. Just what a guy needs in a time of deep depression. A verbal, but solid, kick in the butt.

I developed a certain fascination looking for people my age who were losing their hair, and the ways they tried to disguise the inevitable truth.

There is simply no way to hide the fact that you're going bald. No matter how you arrange what's left of your hair, your scalp is gonna shine through. And, barring the use of an industrial strength hair spray, the slightest hint of a soft summer breeze will destroy your carefully arranged work of hirsute art.

The comb-over is the absolute worst. You've seen it. The perpetrator of this horrific hairstyle starts just above one ear, and combs all his hair over the top of his head. Or, maybe he starts at the back of his neck and combs everything forward, welding it securely in place with a fifth of hair spray.

A former government official from Quebec comes to mind. He appeared to have a comb-over made up of one long ear hair. Once, as he was being interviewed on TV, a strong wind blew his comb-over loose, and a foot-long mass of hair stuck straight out from the side of his head. That piece of televised embarrassment is probably immortalized on the Internet somewhere.

I never tried the comb-over. No matter how hard I wanted to cover the bald spots. Even as they continued to grow both front and back, and as my widow's peak became a distant memory.

By the time I turned thirty, I was seriously considering a toupee. I started reading the ads. Completely undetectable. Swim in it. Look years younger. Feel like a man again. Be all you can be. No, wait. That's the Army slogan.

None of the ads ever mentioned price. To get all the poop on the toop, you had to fill out the little coupon and mail it in. But, those guys in the pictures did look pretty convincing. Were those really toupees? Or did they photograph guys with real hair for those shots? And what about the big breasted blondes in bikinis? In those ads, they were always in doe–eyed admiration of their fully coiffed men.

Larry, a co-worker, was at a state of hair loss even beyond mine. One day, he showed up for work looking just great. But what was it? New suit? Plastic surgery? Wait! Hair. Larry had hair. He was no longer bald.

What the heck? Was it a toop? Or surgery? Maybe those hair-restorers worked after all. I wanted to ask Larry about his new hair. But what if Larry was really sensitive? Maybe he thought no one noticed his new hair. Did he think we had all come down with amnesia? Did he think no one remembered he hadn't always had hair?

Finally, when I ran into Larry in the rest room, I couldn't stand it any longer. "You look great," I told him. "Years younger."

Then I asked, "Is that a toupee?"

Larry nodded sheepishly. "Yes," he said. "I just got tired of looking the way I did. I wanted my hair back. So, I broke down and bought one. Actually, I had to buy two. After you wear one for a day or so, it gets oily and you have to shampoo it. It takes a while to wash and style it. They sell you a little headstand to style it on. Then it has to dry."

Sounded like a lot of work to me. Wash that stupid thing? Every other day?

"So," I continued, curious to know more, "do you wear it all the time? Can you really swim in it?"

"Well, that's what the advertisements say, but I think they're too expensive to risk ruining in that pool water. Besides, swimming is probably overrated as a sport." He smiled and started to walk out.

I wasn't through yet. He really did look younger! This was maybe my chance to get my "Ricky Nelson" look back! "Where did you go to get it?" I asked. "I've been thinking about doing something myself."

Larry came back into the bathroom. "I bought this from Mr. Topper. It's a styling salon in Indianapolis. Check 'em out. And, if you do, mention I sent you. I get two free bottles of toop shampoo for each referral."

I told him I'd do that.

"So Larry," I said. "Do you wear it all the time? Do you wear it to bed?"

Larry got a slight frown on his face. "That's probably the biggest drawback. I guess you could wear it to bed, but it would get wrinkled and smushed. So I take it off when I go to bed."

He hesitated, then grinned. "That's always a shock to your new girl friend. There she is, waiting for you in bed, and then you whip your hair off and put it on that little headstand just before jumping in the sack. That can be a downer, in more ways than one."

He started out of the bathroom again, stopped and turned. "And that wig stand by the bed, it's kind of like having a little faceless man stare at you all night. Kind'a gives your date the willies."

Several years later, after the Company transferred us to Atlanta, there was a guy in the office with about the same degree of hair loss as me. Larry was blond, fairly athletic, and as self-conscious about his receding hairline as I was. We would idly discuss the idea of "hair replacement," (a more dignified way to put it).

When I started losing my hair, all the young girls in department stores began calling me "sir" as I paid for whatever I was buying. That bothered me. Sir? Me? My dad was sir, or mister. Hell, I was the same age as Ricky. And they looked at me like I was Ozzie.

One warm sunny Friday, over lunch, and a couple of martinis, we decided to go to Cosmopolitan Toppers, a salon that advertised in the Yellow Pages. They had a quarter page ad that promised, "completely undetectable, natural looking hair replacement." Look Years Younger!" That last line did it for me.

Lunch was somewhere up on Peachtree. We had two martinis each before lunch, then a third with lunch. Our boss was on the golf course with customers. Larry and I were on our own Mission. It was time for us to become Handsome Young Studs again with a full head of hair ready to blow casually in the wind. We were about to break the bonds of Male Pattern Baldness!

We were feeling no pain as we drove to Cosmopolitan Toppers. It was on a side street, on the north end of Sandy Springs, in a one story concrete block building with one of those trailer mounted signs outside. Blinking lights spelled out, "Cosmopolitan Toppers, Hair Replacement for Gentlemen." We were almost giddy as we parked Larry's Cougar convertible and started inside. The concrete block exterior hid the chrome and glass splendor of the salon inside. This is what Graceland must be like, I thought. Black leather chairs. A red shag rug in the waiting room. Pictures of men, absolutely beautiful men, with full heads of luxuriant hair. And each guy fawned over by a drop dead, knockout blond. Were those guys wearing wigs? That is, Cosmopolitan Toppers? They must be! Surely, the guys that run this place wouldn't practice false advertising! Clearly, we were in the right place.

"Hi, I'm Stan. Can I help you?" We turned to find a young man in black leather coveralls, wearing what appeared to be ballet slippers. His shoulders and back were tanned and muscled under the coverall straps. His thick black hair was fashionably long. A wig? Probably not, I thought. He's probably no more than twenty-four.

Larry and I looked at one another, uncertain as to how to start the process. "Uh, we were thinking about checking out your hair replacement. We saw your ad in the Yellow Pages." Damn. I didn't realize how hard it was to acknowledge to another human being (especially one with great hair) that I was self conscious about going bald. Must be true, I thought. Thinning hair must eat away at your self-esteem.

"Certainly, sir."

Crap; I'm sir to him too?

"Why don't each of you take a chair in the salon".

We took off our jackets and sat in one of the black and chrome salon chairs, facing a mirror that covered the entire wall. Hundreds of bulbs surrounded the mirror, just like in the movies when the stars are getting made up. Stan fussed with our hair, combing it to yield as much of our bare scalp as possible. He put a black one on me, and a blond one on Larry, and worked to comb and weave our own hair into the Toppers. I watched in awe. This was amazing. I looked 10 years younger. Hell, that was Ricky Nelson looking back at me. I was, at that instant, reborn. My youth and self-confidence had been handed back to me. Where was my guitar? Get me to Lazarus. Watch those young clerks fawn over this coiffed God.

I glanced over at Larry, who was smiling into the mirror. His head was tilted up slightly, his jaw firm. A smile played around his lips. We looked at one another in the mirror. Our eyes met. we nodded in agreement. Yep, we were gorgeous. No other word for it.

"By golly, Stan," I said. "This looks great. I'll take it!"

Larry nodded in agreement, turned to Stan, and said, " I'll take mine too. This does seem to make me look a little less old." Larry was an engineer, and tended to reason things out a tad better than me.

Stan was leaning against the beauty table directly behind our chairs. We were facing the mirror, and talked to Stan's image as he stood behinds us.

"A good decision, sirs. You both look great. Younger. More virile. However, I recommend you buy two each. After a day or two, you'll need to wash, style and dry them. You'll need the second to make sure you always look your best. I'll throw in the Styrofoam styling heads for nothing. And, of course you'll need a month's supply of shampoos, sprays, brushes and combs. Let me get you a price."

He walked out to the front. Larry and I were still in awe of the youthful, handsome Men of the World looking back at us from the mirror. Wonder if I ought to wear mine home, I thought. Won't Agnes and the kids be surprised!

Stan came back in. "Well, gentlemen, here's the total. Two Cosmopolitan Toppers each. One free styling head each. The recommended assortment of hair care products for the pieces. And, a complete book of instructions on the care and feeding of your new Toppers. For each of you- $1,486.70.

One Thousand Four Hundred Eighty Six dollars? And Seventy Cents? Good Lord! That was almost two months of house payments. The '68 English Ford I drove to work only cost a little over $400 dollars. Agnes would brain me if I spent that kind of money.

I looked again at my reflection in the mirror. Damn! I am a dead ringer for ol' Ricky, if I squint my eyes and make things a little blurry. I looked over at Larry again. He had a thoughtful look on his face $1,486.70. That's a lot of money. But I kind of look like Ricky Nelson….

Crap! I'm working for the money; I'm smart. I can figure a way to handle it. Besides, Agnes will be thrilled.

I turned to Stan. "You got a deal. I'll take it."

Larry nodded briskly and said, "Me too. I'm going to do it."

We looked at one another and grinned. We were going to be beautiful. And young. Heck, guys with hair got all the best promotions, I told myself.

Stan shook his stylishly coiffed head in acknowledgement and said, "Gentlemen, that is indeed wonderful. Now, let me remove the hairpieces so that I can shave the top of each of your heads."

Wait a minute, I thought to myself, shave my head? I glanced at Larry. He had the same reaction.

"Uh Stan, why do you need to shave our heads?"

Larry looked at Stan. "Yeah, what's that for?"

"Well, sirs (sir again?), the tape has to stick directly to your scalp. I have to get all the hair out of the way of the tape to assure a good fit."

I thought quickly, I didn't want my head shaved! Hell, I didn't want to wear the thing while I did yard work in the hot Atlanta sun. It would be hotter than a wool cap. And I wouldn't wear it on weekends if I were reading out on the deck. I could see that Larry was having second thoughts as well. He had that thoughtful engineer look on his face.

"Stan, I think I'm going to take the weekend and think about this," I said, trying to look serious and carefully thoughtful.

Larry shook his head in agreement. "Let me get back to you as well, Stan. I have to think about the rather permanent commitment I'd be making to my hair."

Stan looked a little crestfallen, as crestfallen as a 24-year old stud with all his hair can manage, anyway.

That was the summer of 1973. I'm still thinking.

We had another guy in the office who surprised us all one day. Wilbur was in his mid 50's, a big man, six foot three, probably 60 pounds over weight. With a close-cropped fringe of white hair around the side of his head, he had been bald for as long as I'd known him.

One day, he showed up at work in a brown Beatle wig. The most ridiculous looking wig I'd ever seen, especially on that big man. Not even real hair. Probably nylon, or some animal hair. Was he serious? Or was this a joke?

He went about his business, met with several of us, and nothing was said about the wig. None of us wanted to hurt his feelings, so we pretended everything was normal.

The next day Wilbur was back in with his wig, but something was different. What was it? I had to ask him.

I went into the tiny office he had next to my equally small office. I pulled up one of the two straight back chairs and said, "Wilbur, I can't help notice you've invested in a....hairpiece. What brought that on?"

Wilbur's face reddened slightly and he smiled. "Ed, I been bald as an egg since I was 23. My wife got after me to try a hairpiece. I found this one at a costume store last week, and thought I'd see what it's like to have hair again. I gotta tell you…it's pretty nice. I must look pretty good, too. Lots of people keep looking at me!"

Wilbur, ol buddy, I bet they do.

"But Wilbur," I said, "something about your 'hair' is different today. I can't put my finger on it. What is it?"

Wilbur looked at me. "Them Beatles let their hair grow down over their ears, and that's how the wig was made. I couldn't stand that mess all over my ears. So I got the wife's pinking shears and cut ear holes in my wig. Feels a world better!"

That was it! Sure enough, there were two oddly shaped and irregular holes for Wilbur's ears to stick out. I did my best to keep a straight face as I left his office.

Wilbur wore his hair for several months. One day, several of us from the office had to fly to Charleston, West Virginia for a meeting. It was a hot, steamy day in the Kanawha River Valley. After the meeting we all piled into the rental car for the trip back to the airport to fly back to Atlanta. We were in suits and ties, wrestling with luggage and briefcases. The plane was a small commuter craft, built to hold probably 20 passengers. It wasn't possible to stand upright in the plane. As we boarded, we had to duck our heads and squirm down the narrow isle to any available seat. The ground support air system was fighting a losing battle against the oppressive heat inside the small cabin. Wilbur managed to fit his height and girth into a seat. I took the seat directly behind him, and struggled to get out of my suit coat. Wilbur was huffing and puffing after the effort to get himself and his luggage stowed under his seat. The back of his suit coat was drenched with perspiration.

As he straightened up, he grabbed the top of his wig, yanked it off with a loud sigh, and mopped the top of his head with his handkerchief. He leaned back in his seat and sighed, "Godamighty! That things hot." He made the trip to Atlanta with his hair tucked into the seat pocket. That was the last time any of us saw Wilbur's wig.

Chapter 10

Almost Heaven? John Denver Obviously Never Bush Hogged West Virginia Hill...

Me and my old 8N on the West Virginia farm

In my next life, I'm going to be a rock star, providing that is, that next time I'm born with some discernable talent. Or maybe I'll be a big-time lawyer. Or a CEO. Any gig where I can make at least a million dollars a year. Hell, I'd even consider inheriting some dough. Just so I can finally live in midtown Manhattan. Fulfill my lifelong dream of living in New York. Maybe the trendy Upper East Side. Perhaps Central Park West. I might even consider a loft in SoHo.

New York City! I love New York. The tall buildings, the nerve center of the entertainment business. Central Park. Even Harlem.

New York. Home of the stars. The movers and shakers. The Center Of Everything!

I fantasize about life in New York. Bumping into Keith Richards at McSorleys. Having a beer with him and discussing the pros and cons of Open G guitar tuning. Dinner at Patroon. At the proper dining hour of 9:00 P.M. At a table next to Gore Vidal and William Styron. Cocktails at the Oak Bar in the Plaza with Donald Trump, who just happened to take the stool next to mine at the bar. Perhaps a casual game of frisbee in Central Park with Brad Pitt and Gwyneth Paltrow. Life would be complete in New York City.

I'd have enough money to hire out everything. Faucet leaks? Call the plumber. He charges $80 an hour and it's a 4 hour minimum? No problem. Chump change. Light bulb out? Call an electrician. Furniture needs to be moved? Not my job. Call the maid. And, while you're up, fix me a drink.

Inevitably, reality slaps me in the face. Here I am, fifty-nine years of age. Still working for a living in Indianapolis. And traveling back to West Virginia as often as we can, trying to keep the family farm from getting completely overgrown.

The farm is located in the rolling hills of Pocahontas County, West Virginia overlooking the Greenbrier River. Just under 100 acres of pasture and woodland. It's been in my wife's family since the mid 1940's. When her father had a stroke last year, the farm became our responsibility. Sell the place? Out of the question. We had to take it over.

It's my wife's, home, and the only really stable home our children ever had. We had to move frequently because of the Fortune 500 company I worked for when our kids were growing up Ohio, Indiana, Georgia, Toronto, Baltimore, Denver. But every summer we'd spend time at the farm with "Gramma and Dede" Jennifer dubbed her Grandfather Dede when she was two. She would try to say Daddy, which is what Agnes called her dad, but it came out Dede, and the name stuck.

Now Dede lies buried in Mountain View Cemetery, near the town of Marlinton. Gramma is in a nursing home, an Alzheimer's patient. And Agnes and I have the farm to take care of.

It was one thing to come to the farm back then. Dede was a natural outdoorsman. He could do anything. A good mechanic, he took care of tractors, mowers, and assorted equipment. He was a trained heavy equipment operator, a carpenter, and a passable electrician. And a veterinarian if he had to be. Took care of his own sheep and cattle. A patient hunter. An excellent shot. The freezer was always full of venison, which Gramma could fix like no one else. Built and maintained his miles of fence by himself. Kept the place mowed and trimmed, in near pristine condition, right up until he had his stroke. Man, I wish I had paid better attention to him when he was trying to get me interested in working on the tractor, or building a fence. For that matter, there were a lot of things I should have paid attention to. Every machine I have back there is designed to chop, rip, cut, grind, maim or kill. Chain saws. Axes. Bush hogs. Rotary tillers. and tractors, notorious for flipping over on these hillsides. But, too late now. Now, if something breaks on the farm or needs doing, there's no one to ask. I have to figure it out for myself. Or ask a neighbor. And you can only do that so many times.

Fortunately, there have been no major disasters yet. No limbs accidentally lopped off by a sharp blade or power saw. No fingers mashed in some hydraulic contraption. And I've managed to get most of the equipment operating with some help from my pal Hubert, a neighbor and retired state road foreman. And Gene, our attorney, a gentleman farmer, and all around good ol' boy, who owns a big spread nearby, is always available to help.

Thankfully, the Good Lord gave me a sense of humor. I seem to have the ability to look at most of my farm catastrophes and find some glint of humor somewhere. And generally I have been able to get most of the farm chores taken care of.

Gene and many of the locals from this area meet every morning at 5:30 for coffee at McCoy's, the local convenience store, grocery, gas station, and hardware store. If you need it, McCoy's probably has it. Their motto, printed on their receipts, is "Fresh Meats, Groceries & Gasoline-Open Seven Days a Week."

Curtis, who runs the water works at the nearby State Prison, is also there. And Lake, who drives the school bus. And Earl, a retired logger. Plus hunters, farmers, truck drivers. They hit McCoy's every morning, weekends included. When I'm back there, I join 'em. They're a good bunch. Down to earth. Good guys. Some, I went to school with years ago. And mornings at McCoy's are entertaining. Folks have a sense of humor. They are sincere. If I need help with machinery, plumbing, electricity, whatever, one of the guys at McCoy's has the skill, and he'll make the time.

To entertain myself after working on the farm all day, I keep a daily journal of my mis-adventures on the farm, and fun at McCoy's. What follows are excerpts from some of the journal entries from the past year or so.

June 30, 2001:

Crap….eighty acres on this place and those stupid groundhogs insist on digging holes right under the house. My pal Hubert, who lives across the road says, "Stuff an oily rag under there. They don't like that." So I found a set of old golf club covers in the barn, soaked 'em with old used oil (no shortage of that on the farm) and stuffed 'em as far under the house as I could. We'll see if Hubert's right. Meanwhile, Ol' One Eye (my trusty single shot .22) goes with me anytime I venture out.

Hubert says I may want to consider some heavier artillery, especially in the evenings. Bears have been spotted in the woods by several of the neighbors, and there is a huge pile of strange looking poop under the cherry tree not far from the house. Looks like bear poop to me, anyway. We'll have to keep a sharp eye out.

Got the battery on the tractor charged up. The bushhog is greased and ready. So tomorrow will test the farming skills of this aging city slicker.

July 1, 2001:

That groundhog must have a degree in psychology. Knows exactly when I'll be working around the barn unarmed. But let me walk out there with Ol' One Eye, and he's nowhere in sight…

No serious injuries to report, just blisters, splinters, and aching joints. That stupid tractor didn't start after all, so tomorrow I'll invest in a new battery. The old one probably dates back to the '60's.

Took several loads of trash up to the landfill near Dunmore. The guys who remodeled the kitchen in the old farmhouse dumped all the old lumber, shingles and carpeting in a pile behind the barn. I was going to burn that pile, but every time I thought seriously about it, I thought what one stray spark could do to that 100 year old, tinder dry barn full of hay bails. So I loaded it in the old pickup and took off.

You cannot believe the wildlife that takes up residence in a trash pile like that: the worlds biggest wasp nest, fire ants, icky looking centipedes, spiders. Made a special trip over to Bobby Taylor' grocery for a couple of cans of hot shot, and Calamine lotion for the ant bites. How can an insect that small bite so hard?

July 2, 2001:
Rats….that %$#@&! tractor…$65 dollars worth of new battery and an hour blown trying to get the old one out. Every nut and bolt rusted…chunks of my skin left on all the sharp edges (is it really necessary to bury a tractor battery that far out of reach?). Got it started and backed out of the barn, and now the hydraulics won't work. So, the bushwacker is useless…Hubert's agreed to come over tomorrow to look at it. Meanwhile, Agnes is all over me for wasting time on the tractor. "Just hire somebody to mow that stupid field so you can help me paint. And I want you to rip those bushes out."

I swear, my life is a living hell back here.

July 3, 2001:

So far, no sign of bears, and that stupid groundhog must have packed up and left. I kept filling his hole with dirt, rocks, motor oil and garlic. Agnes read somewhere that animals don't like garlic. No sign of him today.

Hubert got the hydraulics working on the 8N this morning. Little matter of adding a quart of hydraulic fluid. "That's what that little dipstick on the right side of your tractor is for," he told me.

Guess I oughta read the manual sometime….

July 4, 2001:

Ah man….the two most abundant commodities back here are sweat and poison ivy, and I've had my fill of both. I've been drenched in sweat since 8:30 this morning. Started with some fence repair, then some repair work in the barn and garage. Chopped thistle in the upper field with my Shindaiwa weed whacker. This is nuts. It's 5:30 now. Still 92 degrees, and I have at least two more hours of work based on all the stuff Agnes has scattered around the yard.

July 5, 2001:
Man, what a brutal, brutal day. 100 degrees. Humidity right up there, and gnats! In your eyes, your ears. Spent the entire day outside. Cleaned out the deep cold cellar built into the hillside where Mrs. Simmons kept all the stuff she canned years ago. Jars of canned beans, beets, tomatoes, much of it too old to trust. Mouse poop here and there. Spiders lurking in the rafters. So we cleaned it out; dumped all the canned stuff in buckets, and dumped it down below the barn. We'll have the fattest coons and possums in the county.

November 19, 2001:

The usual crew over at McCoy's this morning at 5:30. Curtis, who works at the state prison below town. Lake, who drives the school bus on the Droop Mountain route, and a truck for the quarry. Earl and Peachy, both retired but who make it to McCoy's for coffee and companionship each morning. Seated on the one high stool by the coffee pots is Gene, gentleman farmer, attorney, and all around good ol boy. First day of hunting season, so a number of hunters stocking up on snacks and pop. All were debating the best places to hunt; all except Gene, that is. He has court today.

Oscar, leaning against the pop machine, isn't hunting today either, " but I got me a nice one last week." Peachy pointed out that deer season didn't start until today. Oscar just smiled and said, "Well, the State's got their schedule, and I got mine."

I asked Gene if I needed a license to hunt on our own land. His answer was no, "not unless you get caught, anyway. But, hell," he said with a grin, "you got the best defense counsel in Pocahontas County!"

My pal Curtis, standing next to Gene, said "buy the license, Ed, be a lot cheaper than this miserable ambulance chaser!" Even Robin, working the early shift at McCoy's, got a kick out of that.

Nov. 20, 2001:

The Charleston paper is full of the usual opening day of hunting season stories. One hunter is killed from falling out of his tree stand. Another hangs upside down for two hours after falling out of his stand. He is rescued by other hunters. And on the front page of the paper, a picture of the Governor with seven stitches over his eye. His new rifle with the scope has more kick than he anticipated!

The best local hunting story is the one about the guy who shot a hole through his transmission yesterday…..in the bank lot in town. He apparently had a loaded gun in his pickup, somehow managed to let it go off. He absolutely denied knowing anything about the incident, even when the deputy pointed incredulously to the bullet hole in the transmission, and the fluid dripping out of the shattered housing onto the pavement.

Bet he didn't have a license to shoot a transmission, either.

Nov. 22, 2001:

Well, ten of us here so far. Both kids, and their children, ranging from four to twelve. The toilet's still working, although it's getting a workout. We're gonna get a new one put in next time back.

The way the old farm house is built, the downstairs john is right off the small family room. So, when you come out, or go in, you have an audience. Tomorrow, I may put a lock on that door. More than one of us has been surprised by another of us opening the door in the midst of our most private activities. Son Matt suggested a fan might be in order, too; as he put it, "a noisemaker".....if you get his drift.

Sept. 23, 2002:

10:53 PM....just got back from Lewisburg, and the Greenbrier Valley livestock auction. Gene invited me to go down with him. He wanted to buy some cows. He wound up buying 37 heifers.

Talk about bedlam! An old fashioned livestock auction at the fairgrounds. Probably 200 serious cattle buyers and wives and girlfriends. Signs all around the bleachers, "Don't spit in the corner. Use the buckets provided." Lot of tobacco chewing goin' on. Gene warned me not to scratch my nose or touch my hat during the actual bidding. "Hell, you might wind up owning the whole damned herd!" We stopped at the bowling alley on the way home to have a beer and watch Peachy's team bowl a few frames. Peachy came over to where Gene and I were sitting, and told us one of his neighbor's was practicing with his bow and arrow. One of his arrows ricocheted off the target and buried itself in his air conditioner. Peachy thinks the unit is toast. Peachy says he's going to get a set of horns to mount on the unit, so the neighbor won't feel so bad.

Sept. 24, 2002:

Man, I hate snakes. I haven't seen a snake on the farm in years….but this evening, I damned near stepped on one. Bet they heard me yell all the way down to Seebert. I almost nailed him with my walk behind bushhog. He came out from under it, clearly determined to get across my foot and into the tall grass. He was a black snake, probably 4-5 feet long. But with snakes, size doesn't matter to me. A twelve foot rattler and a foot long garter snake are all the same as far as I'm concerned.

So I went to the house and got Ol One Eye, (my trusty single shot .22), tramped around behind the barn gingerly, but to my relief, didn't find him. Think I'll bring the 12 guage shotgun next time. Last time I shot a snake with Ol One Eye, I was 12…younger, bolder, and steadier.

Sept. 25, 2002

All I had to do this morning at McCoy's was mention my snake, and the war stories started. One of the fellows said, "We mowed 28 acres of hay over to my place, and killed 28 rattlers. That's a snake per acre!"

Gene told the best story about Jake, the state trapper. One day, Jake came in here with a burlap sack. I knew right away what he had. He said to one of the guys, "Watch this"….and 'accidentally' dropped the sack. That rattler came out right there by the door, and you should have seen the people scatter! Some tried to go out the back door. And there ain't no back door!

Chapter 11

Two Loaves of Bread, a Gallon of Milk, and the Three Bedroom Ranch, Please

Me, Agnes, Jennifer and Matt, about the time I bought our first house.

Saturday morning. Spring of 1969. A bright, sunny day in south central Indiana. Shortly after breakfast, I turned on the TV cartoons for Matt and Jennifer, got in our car, a white un-air-conditioned '67 Buick 2 door, and went off to run my Saturday errands. First a stop at the cleaners, then to the library to drop off an overdue book, then to the real estate office to buy the house, and finally to the grocery. I got back home around 11:30 that Saturday morning, and was unloading the grocery sacks when I casually mentioned to Agnes, "Oh, by the way, I stopped and bought the house."

"You bought a house? What house?" She had a quizzical look on her face.

"The house you took me to look at last night. The ranch on the east side. I thought you wanted it." My stomach was starting to knot.

"Well," she said, "It was all right, but …..you just went out and bought it?"

What was this? Was she second-guessing me? We'd lived in the small mid-western town for nearly five years. First in a tiny, poorly insulated apartment. Later Agnes found a nice three bedroom rambling house on a tree-lined street that we rented. It had a small yard, but plenty of room for the kids to play. If something broke, or a pipe leaked, we'd call the landlord, who lived just across the street.

But Agnes wanted to buy a home of our own. "We're just paying rent! We aren't building up any equity. We need to be building equity."

What the devil was equity, I wondered. Must be an accounting term. Agnes had taken accounting at the Business College in Chillicothe.

So, on some evenings and almost every weekend, Agnes insisted we go look at homes to buy. We walked through house after house after yet another house, with a fawning realtor pointing out the breathtaking beauty of the back yard, or the quaint antique chair rail in the dining room. Meanwhile, my mind was on the pile of papers and phone messages on my little Steelcase desk at the office. Important tasks required my attention! The wheels of industry were mired in the muck of details that demanded action. Action only I could implement. And there I was, trying to feign some slight interest in the "wonderful unfinished basement, which your husband could turn into a comfortable family room in his spare time."

Spare time? Hell, President Johnson had more spare time than me. I had the WesTruck account to manage. I hardly had time to pee! Which school of acting do realtors attend to learn how to seem that excited? Joanne Woodward couldn't hold a candle to the overweight babe I'd followed around last night.

On that fateful Friday evening , I got home from work, ready to collapse in front of the TV with a cold beer to let my head clear. It had been a week full of putting out any number of blazing fires and exploding mini crises. My heart sank as I walked in the door. Agnes had her coat on, and both kids were dressed to go out.

"I thought we'd take the kids out to eat," she said. "And I want us to look at a ranch house on the east side. It's listed at $22,000, and it's a contract sale."

Crap. So much for any thought of a relaxing Friday evening.

"What's a contract sale?" I asked, trying to show some interest. *I could taste that beer. Maybe later.*

"It means we buy the house directly from the owner," she said with mild irritation. She'd told me several hundred times I should read and study about real estate. "Buying a house is a good investment," she insisted.

"You should spend more time worrying about our own home as a business than on that dumb old company."

Sheesh!
We drove out to the far side of town, turned north on a side street; then on to a tree lined cul-de-sac. Small, neat ranch houses were on both sides of the street. On the left; a For Sale sign. On the porch, our smiling realtor.

Are all female realtors overweight, with a couple of chins and rhinestone glasses? Is it a job requirement?

We climbed out of the car, and the realtor, who we'd never met before, started gushing about the kids. "Just wait until you see your rooms," she told Jennifer, who was seven, and Matthew who was four at the time. "And you will have a nice big yard to play in!"

Hell, the car engine hadn't stopped running yet, and this gal had already settled us in. "Actually, we just want to take a quick look," I said.

Agnes shot me a look, and took over. "We'd like to look through the house and understand the terms." She gave me her 'let me handle this' look.

We followed the realtor through the place. Big living room with a fireplace and shag carpet; three bedrooms, two baths. The master bedroom had its own small bath, and there was another bathroom at the end of the hall. The big mirror in that bathroom was cracked. Kitchen, laundry room. Then down to the unfinished (naturally) basement.

Judging from all these unfinished basements, it looked like most homeowners didn't have any more spare time than I did. I noticed a crack in the floor that ran the length of the basement.

Agnes and both kids followed the realtor out into the back yard. I gave the backyard a cursory glance and checked my watch again.

Man, this is taking forever!

Finally, we all gathered in the front driveway, with the real estate lady still hot into her excited pitch. "You'll have wonderful neighbors. Most of them are engineers over at the plant."

Great. I probably work with these guys all day. Eight hours around some of them would have put Molly Brown into a funk. Funeral directors were more light-hearted than the Cooling System Engineering Group.

Agnes took the realtor's card, checked the price again, and promised to get back to her in a few days.

"Don't hesitate too long," she enthused. "A home with this much charm and quiet setting won't last forever."

The For Sale sign was faded, rusty and appeared to have been in place for years. The shrubbery was badly in need of a trim.

This place could still be on the market when I retire.

We left and drove back into town, to Lum's, a new restaurant that specialized in gourmet hot dogs. We didn't talk much about the house. I didn't want to appear too interested, and besides Matt and Jennifer were arguing over the little box of crayons the waitress had left, along with the kiddy place mats designed to keep little minds occupied. Naturally, it wasn't working. Both needed the same red crayon out of the one box of crayons at the same instant.

My business-like recommendation to Matt to use the purple instead was met with a tiny furrowed brow and a, "But Daddy!" He grabbed the red crayon, causing Jennifer to go outside the lines of the barn she was coloring. She turned to Agnes, "Mommy! Look what Matt made me do" Agnes shot me her 'can't you handle anything' look.

I wanted my beer, but I was stuck at a gourmet hot dog place that apparently couldn't spare one extra stinking box of crayons to prevent the outbreak of World War Three at my table. My mind was on a desk full of problems. I had a determined, equity-minded wife glaring at me. I felt the house hunt hanging over my head like a time bomb.

I pondered how I could get at least one of those problems behind me.

Crash! A mug tipped over. Liquid sloshed all over the table. I heard Matt's anguished cry, "She did it, Mommy!" I grabbed the napkin box just as Jennifer let out a howl, holding up her ruined place mat.

Agnes grabbed the napkins from me and took control. Chocolate milk dribbled onto my khakis and into my right shoe. Matt took advantage of the confusion and grabbed the red crayon.

Then came Saturday morning.

That Saturday morning, I had a mission. I was going to TAKE CHARGE. I was the breadwinner, right? I worked a demanding job that required uninterrupted blocks of time to concentrate. I could not spend many more nights and weekends running helter-skelter all over Indiana looking at houses. I was a busy, important man. A decisive, action oriented executive. I was capable of putting my foot down to TAKE ACTION. So, I left the house in our '68 Buick Special; V6, stick shift, AM radio and no A/C. Our first new car. We'd been all the way to Texarkana in that car to see the in-laws. We were really starting to "See America" because I worked for a fine company that gave me two full weeks of vacation.

At the library, I easily blew an hour. Then up to the cleaners to drop off my green wool jacket and stained khakis. I picked up a black suit I'd paid $19 for at a discount store near the Ohio State campus. It was my interview and funeral suit. The dress code at work was buttoned-down shirt, tie, and coat; preferably dark. All the Harvard MBA's wore buttoned-down shirts and striped ties, and I did my best, with our limited budget, to dress the part.

Then it was off to the real estate office to buy the house. When I told the overweight agent I wanted to buy the place, her jaw dropped, but she recovered. "What would you like to offer?"

Offer? What the heck? The advertised asking price was $22,000?

"The guy is asking $22,000 dollars, so we'll take it," I said.

Come on, I haven't got all day. I still have to get to the grocery and mow the yard.

"You…..you'll take it? $22,000 dollars?" She looked shocked. I wondered why?
"Yeah" I said. "What do I have to do next?"

She just sat there staring at me. Finally, she shook her head, as if to clear her mind. She looked confused. I wondered how long she'd been selling houses?

"Well, well," she said, shuffling through the papers on her desk, "let me find the offering from the seller. You'll have to sign that."

She stopped and looked up at me, "22,000 dollars….right?" She cocked her head. Her eyes fixed on mine.

What the heck is wrong with her memory? Why can't she keep that number straight?

I sighed, "Yeah, $22,000 dollars. And 10 percent down, right?" I tried to sound crisp and businesslike. "I'll write you a check for $2,200 dollars." Agnes told me Friday night we had just over $2000 in our savings account.

She was still searching through her stack of papers, and not having much luck. Apparently, organization is not her strong suite. I thought I could see the color begin to drain from her face as she searched for the right paperwork, her hands shaking slightly. She seemed to be hyperventilating.

"Oh no no no," she said, "where the hell IS IT?" Good Lord, I thought, is she all right?

"Here it is," she cried, with a shout of relief. She actually crossed herself.

She jerked the document out of the stack and shoved them at me, then almost stabbed me with her pen as she thrust it into my hand. "You just sign right here, and the house is YOURS!" Her breathing started to return to normal.

"And just put your initials by the price, just $22,000"

I signed, initialed, looked at her importantly, "What else?"

Her realtor personality started radiating from behind the rhinestone glasses. With a big smile she said, "That's all for now. I'll contact the seller, and we'll get all the closing papers started. We can probably close next week."

Close? What does that mean.

I walked out into the late morning sunshine, relieved that I had solved my problem. After she closed the door, I wondered why she was yelling. Maybe she'd stubbed her toe.

"You just went out and bought a house?" Agnes stood stock still, watching me as I unloaded the grocery sacks.

"The ranch we looked at last night. I thought you wanted it," I said, not sure I wanted to meet her steady stare.

"You bought it? Just like that? Without discussing it?" She shook her head; then looked at me. "Did you sign anything?"

I gave up unloading the groceries. "Yeah, I signed something. She says we can close in a week or two." My throat tightened. I started to panic.

"How much did you offer?" Agnes asked.

I was afraid I was going to throw up. All those questions, questions I should have thought of. "Well, they were asking $22,000 dollars, so that's what I offered." Now I was starting to hyperventilate. "It was the price, you know."

"YOU JUST GAVE THEM THEIR PRICE? she shouted, her hands up to her face. "You NEVER give them what they ask for. You go low, and they counter the offer. Don't you know anything? You just met their offer? Did they accept?"

I told her I didn't know. I wanted to disappear.

Why can't I just have heart failure now?

"What about the broken mirror in the bathroom, and the crack in the basement? Did you make the offer conditional on fixing those things?"

The blank look on my face was all the answer she needed.

She kept up the interrogation. Finally, she turned and looked out the kitchen window; and let out an exasperated sigh, "Can we even afford it?"

Now I panicked. Completely. "I thought you had that figured out! Why else would we even look at the place?"

Agnes closed her eyes; signaled me to be quiet, and turned to get a pen and some paper. In a quiet, controlled voice she said, "Let's figure out if we can make the payments." After about fifteen minutes of work, the conclusion was clear. We could not afford to buy the house. Out of the question. Then, one other realization hit us both at the same time. We'd have to have a second car! The house was out on the edge of town; Agnes worked as a dental hygienist. The kids were starting into school activities. No way could we get to all the commitments with one car.

So, now I had to call the realtor and get out of the deal.

I explained I had made a mistake. Hadn't talked to my wife. Hadn't done a budget. Hadn't figured on a second car. Couldn't go through with the deal. Sorry. I asked her to keep us in mind. We really did want to buy a place!"

There was a long silence on the other end of the phone. When the realtor started to speak, her voice was as cold as ice. "Mr. Friel, you signed a valid offer for twenty-two thousand dollars. The seller has accepted your offer. He has your ten percent good faith money. You bought the house. If you try to back out now, you will lose your ten percent down, and the seller has a right to hold you to the deal."

There was no negotiating with that tone of voice. I had a vision of the Wicked Witch of the West on the other end of the phone. I didn't know what to say. I mumbled something and hung up.

I turned to Agnes. What was that look on her face. Anger? No. It was a look of fear. This time I had really done it.

We spent the rest of the day alone with our thoughts, going about a few chores half-heartedly.

We were scheduled to go to a party that night at the home of one of the Application Engineers, a BYOB party. Normally, I'd take a six-pack of PBR for Agnes and me to last us through the evening. But, on this night, with a $22,000 problem hanging over us, and the need for a second car, I knew a six-pack was not the answer. We were going to need something stronger to help us forget, and to get us through the night without a nervous breakdown, or a fistfight.

We weren't big drinkers, but I went to Tom's Discount Liquors and bought a bottle of Jack Daniels. We really didn't get into the party. We just tried to forget the mess we were in. Or, rather, the mess I had created.

Agnes and I went through that whole bottle that night. We killed that bottle. Just the two of us.

It didn't even faze us. At the end of the evening, we were still cold sober, every nerve raw with the thought of what we were facing.

We got home around 1:00AM, wide awake and focused on our $22,000 house, our need for a second car; our shattered budget, and our impending financial disaster.

I couldn't even think about the now trivial problems on my little Steelcase desk.

The next few weeks passed in a blur. I tried to put the house out of my mind. But the realtor had other ideas. She sent me the forms to fill out to get financing, and kept the pressure on so we could move on with closing. I wanted to put the house out of my mind, but Agnes pressed me. "Get on with the move. We're committed."

One evening, I took Matthew with me to our new house. I put Matt in the car and we drove out. I did some measuring that evening, to see where things would fit. I saw that Matt had made friends with two kids who had wandered up the driveway.

Well, there's a bright spot. At least there are kids in the neighborhood.

Matt ran into the empty living room. "Daddy, Daddy! Guess what?" He jumped up and down with excitement. "Daddy! The boy next door has a pig!" My heart sank.

God in Heaven, don't let it be true. Not pigs? Not next door. Why in hell didn't I check this place out better?

I looked at Matt. "How many? Did you actually see them?" I had visions of my Dad coming to visit, and eyeing the hogs rooting in the yard next door. I could see him wrinkling his nose and shaking his head at the idea of his son living next door to a pigsty.

Yeah Daddy! I saw him! He's got a little Ferris wheel in his cage!"

I almost cried with relief. The boy next door had a guinea pig.

Maybe this'll work out after all.

I also started to ask the guys at the office about a used car. Boy, it's just amazing how people can smell a buyer in trouble.

Dick, who had the Steelcase desk in the row behind me, told me he had a car to sell. "Great little car. Just the thing for your wife to use as a second car," he said brightly. "Got it out in the parking lot. Wanna take a look?"

We walked out into the spring sunshine, and down to the far end of the lot. Dick stopped by a small, strange looking foreign car. He put his hand on the roof and patted it like his favorite pet.

"This is it", Dick said. "An English Ford. Little four cylinder engine, straight stick on the floor. Runs forever on a tank a' gas. Painted it myself. Want to take a drive?"

I looked at the car. It was small. A two door, painted green, and trimmed in black. By the look of the brush marks, it had been hand painted. I walked around it. There was a piece of chain link fence where the grill should have been. I looked at Dick. He furrowed his brow when he saw my questioning look. He said, "I had to do a little repair work on the radiator when Barb hit the garage wall. Damned brakes gave out. She busted that grill all to pieces! But that little piece of fence don't look too bad, now does it? I rebuilt the brakes myself, so it's in pretty good shape for what you want to do."

He smiled when I asked to take it around the block. First time I'd ever driven an import.

When I pulled back in, I asked him why he wanted to sell it.

He grinned and said, "Ol' man Baker gave me a little raise last review. "

Harvey Baker supervised the Sales Engineering group.

"Think I'll be able to get a loan at the Credit Union for a used Corvair. Barb wants a convertible, and there's one over at Bob's Used Cars. Nice little yellow job. I asked Bob to hold it for a coupla days."

Great! Dick's buying a car for his wife for fun, to upgrade her life style. My back's against the wall, and I gotta buy a ride for my wife, because I was stupid enough to buy an entire house without THINKING!

"Well, it doesn't seem like a bad car, Dick. How much?"

Dick shook his head and grinned. "Tell you what Ed, you're a friend, and I'll make you a good deal." *God help me. Another good deal just handed to me. Has the entire world got my number?*

My sphincter tightened as he pretended to think of a price. "I'll let you have that car for $160 dollars," Dick said, a hopeful expression on his face.

My mind raced. I calculated what I was making, minus what our new house payments would be, the student loans, the one gas credit card....hell, I had no choice. No sense shopping for a used Corvette, or something fun to drive. I needed transportation. I didn't have an extra $160 dollars, but I did have an urgent need for a second car. I told him I'd take it.

Probably should have asked Agnes, but why worry her? For once, I was right. I told her I'd gotten a good deal on a second car. When she heard the price, she closed her eyes and said, "Thank you Lord."

Sure hope she likes the paint job, I thought.

Several weeks later, we closed on the house. We wiped out our meager savings account with the balance due on the down payment. My mind was a blur as I signed the papers, committing me to 30 years of what seemed like an unthinkably rich monthly mortgage.

The realtor was her old self, gushing about the "marvelous buy" and the "quaint country setting" of our new home.

Is a weed-infested cornfield bordering the backyard "quaint?"

She had one piece of good news, "The seller knows about the broken mirror in the bathroom, and he's going to have that replaced."

" I really appreciate that," I said. Then I added tentatively, "We noticed the basement floor has a crack in it. We'd like some help in having that redone."

The realtor seemed to stiffen in her chair. The smile changed to a grimace. "Mr. Friel, the crack in the floor is normal for a home of this vintage, in this area. I can assure you it's not an issue for you to worry about."

I glanced at Agnes. She shot me a look that said 'great time to bring up the floor, stupid'...now that you OWN THE HOUSE!'

As it turned out, buying that house was the right thing to do. We worked on it, fixed it up, got the yard in pretty good shape. Then, almost a year to the day we bought it, I got a promotion and a transfer to Atlanta. I was going to be a Regional Manager, and travel the southern states. We sold the place in about a month, and made a nice little profit. Had enough money now for a down payment on a nice new two story on a wooded lot in the Atlanta suburb of Roswell.

The Old Man was impressed with both my promotion, and the new house. I overheard him tell Mom one day, "That Eddie's a pretty smart boy. Look at this fine house. He's pretty shrewd to afford a place like this."

Sure wish Agnes had heard that!

Chapter 12

So, I Ain't the Sundance Kid

As Robert Redford plays him in that great 70's movie, "Butch Cassidy and The Sundance Kid, " the Sundance Kid is the fastest gun in the West, and the best shot. Never misses. He was awesome. In the movie, Redford/Sundance shoots the belt buckle off the bad guy's gun belt without harming a hair, or a navel, on him. Just jerks that pistol out of his holster and fires, without aiming. Fanning the hammer of his Colt .45, Sundance shoots a silver dollar out of the air, and hits it five more times before it hits the ground. Makes it look easy.

I grew up watching all the old cowboy movie stars: Roy Rogers, Gene Autry, Lash LaRue, Tim McCoy, The Lone Ranger. Any one of them was every bit as good a shot as Sundance. All those guys got their man with one shot, without aiming, generally while astride a galloping horse. And Gene, Roy, Lash, Tim - always shot the gun out of the bad guy's hand. They almost never drew blood with a bullet. Lash was pretty good with a bullwhip too.

All of them had pretty fancy rigs, wide leather gun-belts, fancy-tooled holsters. And Colt .45 pistols. Roy Rogers had a set of gold .45's. The Lone Ranger used silver bullets for his two silver Colts with ivory handles. Old Gene carried just a simple gunmetal blue one with wooden handles.

I wanted one of those "real" Cowboy guns from the time I was 8 years old. One Christmas, I was probably 10, I prayed for a Colt Cowboy .45.- a realistic looking plastic toy out of the Sears catalog. A black one with white plastic handles and a longhorn steer molded on the handle. I prayed hard for that plastic pistol.

Christmas morning came. Just shirts, socks and underwear. I was mad at God for weeks.

I finally got my real Cowboy .45 two years ago. I saw the one I wanted standing in line at the grocery store in a magazine called, "Cowboy Shooting."

Have you noticed the sheer number of magazines available these days? Pick a subject, and there's a magazine devoted to it. Can't find a magazine on your hobby of collecting toenail clippings? You're not looking hard enough. Or, better yet, start one! Charge $8.95 a copy. Use a lot of pictures, and start looking for a place in the Hamptons. You're on your way to making a million bucks. People these days will buy a magazine about anything. Just spend 20 minutes in the magazine area of Borders, or on the checkout line at the grocery. I added "Cowboy Shooting" to my cart that day.

I got a good deal from a friend who knew a gun dealer. The Cowboy .45 cost me $179.85 over the trade allowance on the old single shot shotgun I'd bought at a garage sale. And because you couldn't very well carry your Cowboy .45 in your pocket, I sent off for a gun belt and holster advertised in "Cowboy Shooting." The ad said it was identical to the one John Wayne wore in all his movies. .

My Cowboy .45 was just like Ol' Gene's, gunmetal blue, with a smooth wooden handle. Nothing fancy about it. No carved ivory handles. No gold finish. Just an everyday cowboy gun. Me and Gene. Just a couple of fast drawin', straight shootin' gunslingers.

On Saturday, I went to a gun store on the north side of Indianapolis and bought a box of .45 caliber bullets. The box of 24 cost me almost $30.00. More than one dollar for each stinking bullet. That got my attention. Hell, no wonder those old time cowboys got their man with one shot! An extended gunfight would have forced a gunslinger into bankruptcy.

Soon, my gunfighter rig had arrived. Big wide belt. Cartridge loops for those one dollar bullets. A tooled leather holster. I strapped that rig on, stuck my cowboy pistol in the holster, and walked over to the full-length mirror in our bedroom. Man, did I look the part.

Look out, Liberty Valance, Deadeye Ed's hit town. Hell, Eastwood couldn't look any more cool or deadly.

I was a formidable, armed and dangerous gunfighter. Except for the white tee shirt. And the checkered Bermudas. And the dock shoes with no socks.

I tried a quick draw, crouched down, stared squarely in the eye of my mirror image, and whipped out my deadly .45. Tried to anyway. The holster was so stiff, the gun wouldn't come out; All I managed was to pull the pistol up to about chest level, the gun still in the holster, the belt riding ridiculously up my tee shirt.

This fast draw stuff would take some practice.

I'd have a pair of jeans on next time I strapped on the rig.

Couple of weeks later, we went back to our West Virginia farm. One hundred acres of pasture and woods. Lots of groundhogs, raccoons, deer, bear. And it's legal to carry a handgun on your own property. I resolved never to go out without strapping on my gunfighter rig.

My wife had her own thoughts. "Why are you putting that stupid gun on to go out and trim the hedge? Think a tribe of Indians is going to ride up out of Seebert? If the neighbors drive in and see you with that thing, they're going to think you need therapy."

She obviously failed to realize the awesome power of the Colt .45, or the True Grit of us Cowboy Shooting devotees.

The next evening, when I walked out to the barn, I spotted the raccoon. A big raccoon, sitting on a fencepost, his back to me, grooming himself. And there I was, without my cowboy gun. Living proof I should have never listened to my wife's protests.

I carefully backed away, so as not to scare the raccoon. These stupid coons were destructive, digging under the barn, getting into the garbage. Some may even be rabid. I was doing West Virginia a favor by ridding the farm of these pests. I headed for the house, and my cowboy gun. It was mine. It would be my first kill with my .45. I strapped on my rig, and picked up 3 cartridges that had fallen out of the box. I hadn't filled the loops on my gun belt with bullets yet. Just picked up the three loose ones. Besides, I was a Shootist. I was only going to need one. Just like Roy and Gene. One shot. No sense wasting ammo.

As I walked back to the barn, I loaded the 3 cartridges into the cylinder of the gun. I thought to myself, this was just how Roy and Hopalong loaded their guns. I was living the Legend!

I eased around the barn, and there he was. That big, stupid raccoon was still grooming himself. He had no idea I was anywhere on the planet.

I raised my cowboy gun, cocked the hammer, took a John Wayne stance, and pulled the trigger. The explosion was deafening. A foot of flame roared out of the muzzle, and that raccoon leaped straight up in the air. Good Lord! Did I miss him? How the hell did that happen? Yep. Missed him. That raccoon came down on the ground, landing on his feet, and looked around frantically to find the source of that noise.

I had 2 shots left. The raccoon was crouched in the high grass, staring at me. This time, I assumed the two-handed Clint Eastwood stance, aimed carefully, and fired. BOOM! The pistol jumped in my hand. My eyes closed inadvertently. I opened them quickly, fully expecting to see the raccoon lying dead in the grass. No such luck. That stupid coon was still crouched in the grass, looking at me.

One shot left. I couldn't miss this time. There was no way I could walk back to the house empty handed, the smoking gun in my hand. Roy and Gene would be shaking their heads in disgust.

I crouched down. Held the gun as steadily as I could and aimed at the widest part of the coon I could see. Surely I'd hit something.

You guessed it. Missed again. That coon is probably still laughing his striped ass off. My Old Man was an officer in the Federal Prison Service. He had to qualify at least twice each year on the range with handguns, rifles, and machine guns. As I walked back to the farmhouse, I remembered his words, as he watched TV. "Look at Roy, shooting that gun out of that guys hand! That's impossible! Roy would have a better chance actually hitting the guy if he threw his gun at the bad guy!"

Maybe I'll try that next time.

Chapter 13

Why I Won't be Dining at Texas Roadhouse; or, The Night Ol Willie Sang the Same Damn Song for Three Hours

If you are a fan of country music or ol' Willie, you may want to skip this chapter.

Let me state one thing right away, for the record, about Texas Roadhouse. The food is probably fabulous. The service may be the best in town. Texas Roadhouse may well be the choice of the pickiest gourmets across America. I have no beef with their food. I've never tasted it. I can't give you a bum steer about their service. I've never experienced it.

My issue with Texas Roadhouse, and several other chains, is their choice of music.

Pull up in the parking lot of a Texas Roadhouse Restaurant, and you can hear the music from a block away. Hillbilly music. Played at about 8.0 on the Richter scale.

Hillbilly music. Call it Country & Western, if you prefer. I can't stand it. I'm not just talking about bluegrass or Earnest Tubb. I'm talking about all of it. Brooks and Dunn, Alan Jackson, somebody named Twain. I won't listen to any of 'em.

I won't let Country music be played in my car. The Pope himself couldn't get me to tune in a Country station if he hitched a ride in my fire engine red Chrysler 300M. So, it's not likely I'd enter a Texas Roadhouse, or any other establishment if they play hillbilly music.

Let me say at this point that I am not demeaning hillbillies. After all, I am one. Proud of my West Virginia heritage. I am not for one-second making light of the good folks from Kentucky or West Virginia. Just the infernal music that some say originated there.

I haven't always felt this way. I used to like hillbilly, or Country and Western. Taught myself to play guitar listening to Johnny Cash. Thought the early

Everly Brothers were fantastic. Waylon was one of my guitar heroes, since he played with Buddy Holly. And there's Willie Nelson, Don Williams, many others. And the great songs. Story songs. Songs with a message. Love gained. Love lost. Babies dying (just listen to Little Jimmy Dickens do Heaven's Little Angel). Dogs run over. Daddy's in jail. If you listen to Country music, you will hear songs about every imaginable human tragedy.

I used to get my guitar out and play Johnny Cash songs at BYOB parties when we lived in Atlanta during the '70's. Problem was, I didn't sound much like Johnny Cash, and occasionally someone would point that out to me. "Damn Ed, that doesn't sound like "I Walk The Line" the way ol' Johnny does it." That hurt my feelings.

So I set out to write my own country songs. I figured there was no way someone could say, "that doesn't sound like an Ed Friel song" if I actually wrote it.

I must have written 300 songs over a period of 10 years or so. Some of them were pretty good, according to friends who heard them. Of course, it helped that those friends were under the influence of lots of cheap booze when they rendered those judgements.

I did some of my best writing in sales meetings at Company headquarters. A particular Marketing VP would get up in front of an audience of field sales reps (I was a Regional Sales Manager) and start his hour long presentation supplemented with several hundred Mylar slides. Five minutes into his talk, my eyes would glaze. I'd get out a tablet of paper, and start to compose. Brilliant stanzas like:

> The buttercup bouquet of love
> Is all I tried to find
> But the heartaches grow like ragweed
> In the hayfields of my mind

And so on.

My Cousin Dan was (and is) a huge Country and Western music fan. Dan was a Captain with one of the major airlines and, by his own admission, had just four interests in life: airplanes, beer, good lookin' women, and Country and Western music. When he wasn't flying, he'd get a six-pack, drive out to Washington National Airport, and park near the end of the runway. Watching airplanes land and take off, he'd sip on a PBR and listen to Country music.

When my travels took me to Washington, I'd spend the night at Dan's house. We'd go down to the bar in his finished basement, drink beer and listen to Country music.

One night, about midnight, deep into a case of Pabst Blue Ribbon, Dan put on a Ronnie Milsap tape. Ronnie is a blind country singer/songwriter, and has written some really memorable stuff. . That night, we listened to one of Ronnie's best, "Back on My Mind Again." It's a song about a guy losing his best girl, and trying to forget her by going on a trip. But like the song suggests, she keeps coming back on his mind. Dan and I had enough beer to feel melancholy, and both of us started to get teary eyed. Funny what copious quantities of alcohol will do to otherwise pretty normal guys.

I looked at Dan and said something. Dan's head snapped up. He looked at me and said, "Ed, that's the most memorable thing I've ever heard you say. You need to write that down and turn it into one of your songs!"

I stared at Dan, trying to remember what I had just said. I couldn't think. My alcohol-numbed mind was a complete blank. So I said to Dan, "Really? What was it I just said?"

Dan looked at me, his eyes not quite focusing. Then looked at the ceiling, got a goofy grin on his face and said, "Hell Ed, now I can't remember what you just said. But it was brilliant. If you can remember and write that down, it'd be the start of an award winning country song."

Wonder if that ever happened to Willie?

Yup, I was a big fan of Country & Western music. Wrote the stuff. Played it on my guitar. Had my car radio set to several C & W stations. Knew the songs that were at the top of the charts, and the artists who sang them. Even hired Tommy Jennings (Waylon's brother) one year to perform at a company function. Had a hand in bringing Little Jimmy Dickens to a convention in the '70's. I even carried on a conversation with Little Jimmy after the show in the men's room as we were relieving ourselves at adjoining urinals. Talked about the fact we'd both grown up in West Virginia.

That night at the convention, Little Jimmy did his song "Heavens Little Angel." It's about a daddy whose little baby daughter dies. It's a blue ribbon, triple tear jerker, one of the saddest, most morbid songs ever written. Little Jimmy came out on the darkened stage where a prop tombstone had been set up, complete with flowers. He took off his big cowboy hat, knelt down, placed a teddy bear on the "grave" and began to sing. I swear, he'd have brought tears to the eyes of Osama Bin Laden with that song.

So, what happened with Country music and me?

It all fell apart the night I went to a Willie Nelson concert and ol' Willie sang the same damned song for almost three hours. It happened right after I was transferred to a new job in Denver. I was living in an apartment while my wife stayed behind in Baltimore trying to sell our house. I was pretty much free to do whatever I wanted. My new boss, Bill, had 2 tickets near the front, for a Willie Nelson concert. His wife didn't want to go. Bill knew I was a Country music fan. He asked me, as he put it, to go as his date. I accepted. Bill was right. Our seats were great. Five rows back, near the center. Great view of the stage. Grady Martin was accompanying Willie on lead guitar. Hell, talk about a bonus. I had listened to Grady Martin for years. He was one of the legendary guitar pickers on the Grand Old Opry. I would have come just to see and hear ol' Grady play.

We settled back to wait for the show to start. About to see Willie in person. With the rare opportunity to see Grady Martin. Five rows from the stage. The Coors we'd had the good sense to buy was cold and satisfying. Me with my new Boss. Life was good.

The show started. There he was! Ol' Willie himself. He had that classic guitar with the hole busted in it. Red neckerchief, dirty jeans, black tee shirt, ponytail, three-day growth of beard. Just like in all the pictures.

Over to his right, Grady Martin himself. Heavier than I would have thought. With kind of a sea captain's cap, sans-a-belt slacks, open necked white shirt. Hell, he looked like he'd just flown in from Sarasota.

On Willie's left, his sister on piano. Not a bad lookin' gal, in her tight fittin' jeans and cowboy hat.

Willie didn't say much, just started with one of his songs. The crowd, including me, went wild.

I leaned over to Bill, "This is great I've always wanted to see Willie. And these seats couldn't be better!" Bill shook his head and grinned, lost in Willie's music. It was just after 8:00.

My man Willie kicked it off with "Me and Paul." I was completely blown away by actually seeing Willie perform, and watching Grady play that Gibson guitar so effortlessly. Man, I was livin' large.

"Seven Spanish Angels" next. Then, "I'm Movin' On." This was great. Wished I'd been smart enough to buy two cups of Coors.

"Hello Walls." "Slow Movin' Outlaws." The songs continued without a break. "City of New Orleans." Wondered what time it is? Hmm….8:35.

"In the Jailhouse Now." "Everything is Beautiful." By now, I was beginning to wonder; did this show have an intermission?

"Faded Love." "Good Time Charlie's Got the Blues." Willie, I thought to myself, this is really great, but candidly, if I was listening to all this on CD, I'd hit fast forward through a couple of those songs. "Texas on a Saturday Night." Good Lord, I was starting to think that Willie only knew one lead guitar bridge pattern. Did they really all sound alike, or was I getting too critical in my old age?

"Whiskey River." 9:20.

Damn, Willie, I don't know about you, but I need a break. I need to pee, get some fresh air, take an Excedrin, and reload on Coors.

This was turning into a long evening.

"On the Road Again." "Angel Flying Too Close to the Ground." "Stay a Little Longer."
No, please. I've stayed long enough. I've heard enough.

My head started to throb. I couldn't keep my eyes off my watch. I was ready for this to end. I mean, it had been great…or good. But what ever happened to the axiom, "leave the stage when they still want more?" "Night Life." "Without a Song."

Gee, that would be neat. No more songs!

I really couldn't take any more of that doo doodo doodo doo doop doop guitar thing that Willie did in EVERY song.

Good Lord, is that annoying, or what?

I wanted to get that guitar in my hands just long enough to smash it to smithereens.

"Summertime." "Always on My Mind."

Shit, Willie, now I'll never be able to get you off my mind.

That was it. This had gone on far too long. It was 10:40. I wanted to pee, now. I wanted a beer. I wanted to get away from the madness. I wanted to get OUT OF HERE.

Much as I used to love Willie, every song now sounded the same. I had not come to hear Willie sing the same song for three hours. But God in Heaven, that was what happened. Every damned song sounded just like the last one.

I swore an oath to myself; if I survived, I'd never listen to Country and Western again Never. Ever.

"Mona Lisa." The Party's Over.

God, if it only could be.

I now considered murder, or suicide. I had to get out.
God in Heaven, hear my prayer. Let this end!

Finally nearing 11:00, Willie announced he would end with "Blue Eye's Cryin' in the Rain." My prayer had been answered. As soon as he finished, I could pee, buy a Coors, and try to get the pain in my head under control.

Blue Eye's ended....and the crowd went wild. My heart sank. With all that applause and screaming, Willie and Co. would feel obliged to come back for an encore. The last thing I needed.

I wanted to stand up, turn to the crowd, and say, "No....please...No! Don't encourage him."

Naturally, he did come back. For three encores. Three more of the same damned sound alike songs. The same machine gun guitar solos. Doop pee doo pee doo doop doop.

Finally, the lights came up. Willie and Co. left the stage.

I was a wreck, headache, nerves frayed, but at last free to go. Bill turned to me and said, "That was just great, wasn't it? We had the best seats in the house, didn't we?"

I forced a smile and said something agreeable through clenched teeth. But I had already fiercely resolved to cancel out all the preset Country stations on my car radio. I swore that never again would hillbilly music be played in my presence. Not in my car. Not on any occasion. Not for anything.

It's been over 15 years, and I still can't stand Country and Western. If somebody offered me front row tickets to see Dolly Parton perform June Carter's Greatest Hits stark naked, I wouldn't go. No damn way. She'd probably sound exactly the same after the first three songs too.

Yeah, Ed, but it's Dolly Parton, and she performs stark naked!

Sure, but it's still hillbilly and I've already seen a naked woman.

Chapter 14

You Sure This Ain't Greyhound?

If all of your airline travel has been in the last 15 to 20 years, you're used to it. The crowded airplanes and the overweight, baggy shorts clad, backward baseball cap wearin', duffel bag totin', high-top gym shoed yahoos, with everything they own in assorted carry-on bags, any one of which is in violation of airline travel policy. But the airlines seldom, if ever, enforce their own policy for carry-on bags.

You probably have a perfect mental picture of that overweight guy in 15B, trying to jam a 36-inch bulging duffel bag into the 24 inch compartment directly over your head. The bare midriff between his tank top and cut-offs brushes up right against your cheek. His tattoos are on every exposed body surface. Topped off by a shaved head, a goatee, and a ring tastefully piercing his eyebrow.

That's way different than how it used to be. I remember my first airplane flight. It was probably 1962. My grandmother and I were going to fly to Jacksonville to visit my favorite aunt, who was the mother of my favorite cousin, Kathy. Kathy was gorgeous, a blond with a sunny personality. I'd see her each summer at my grandparents' farm when all the relatives gathered for a reunion. God, she got more beautiful each year.

Mom had asked me to get off from my summer jobs to accompany Grandma to Florida. She was going to stay for a few weeks. I'd only stay for a few days, then fly back to work at the paper mill where, I hoped to earn enough money for my junior year at Ohio State.

Making sure Grandma got to Florida safely had an added bonus. I'd also see Kathy for a few days. Could I get off from my job? Of course I could do it.

Mom bought the tickets from the travel agent in town. We were actually going. No paper mill drudgery for a week. And glorious days under the same roof with Kathy.

The big day! I put on my only suit, with a white shirt and tie Mom and Dad drove us to the airport. We checked in at the counter, and went to the gate. Most of the people in the airport were dressed up in their Sunday best. . In the early 60's, you got dressed up to fly. And, there was an excitement in the air. The fortunate few were going to fly to fascinating destinations. The rest were there to see them off, and maybe to see that new marvel of the modern age, the jet airliner. Most of the airplanes flying then were still propeller driven.

Our flight to Jacksonville was on a TWA Constellation. A big, tri-tailed, four engine propeller job. The stewardesses were dressed in suits and tasteful little hats. The pilots in the cockpit their uniform jackets on. The flight engineer, seated behind the co-pilot facing a huge panel of dials and instruments, had his jacket on too. The crew's formal dress code gave me, and probably the rest of the passengers, added re-assurance. It signaled they clearly had no intention of getting those fine uniforms dirty in some flaming plane crash.

Our flight to Jacksonville was about half full. Grandma and I had a row of seats to ourselves. Shortly after takeoff, the young and very professional stewardess served us a full meal; chicken, potatoes au gratin, green beans with those little onion rings, bread, and coffee, tea or milk. On white cloth napkins. And this was what it was like just in tourist class in those days. I could only imagine what it was like for the folks in first class.

Into the '70's, flying was an experience I looked forward to. Generally, there was an open seat next to you. You had your choice of window or aisle. Reasonably good food. Attractive stewardesses. And one dollar martinis. On a long flight to the west coast, it was possible to get several hours of work done, have a couple of drinks with dinner, and read a good book. All with plenty of legroom and a place for your briefcase in the empty seat next to you.

Fast forward to today. Every flight is over booked. Surly desk agents won't make eye contact. Airports are jammed with humanity. Most look like they just rolled out of bed to get to the airport. Unshaven. Dressed for yard work. Pulling a U-Haul sized suitcase on wheels plus a backpack or a bulging shoulder bag. And they intend to carry-on all of it. Do they even consider checking those bags to their destination? Are you kidding? And risk losing all their luggage, and its precious contents which I can only imagine to be a complete collection of Disco Hits of the 80's on 8-track.

Nine times out of ten now, you get jammed into the middle seat. The biker with the shaved head is on your left. A Jenny Craig dropout is on your right. He's yelling into his cell phone. She's gobbling French fries out of a McDonalds bag between her knees.

What happened to turn air travel from one of life's small pleasures to hell on earth? The Democrats. Jimmy Carter. De-regulation. The idea to make air travel affordable not just for business executives or the wealthy, but for the little guy.. Open it up for everybody. Make flying as inexpensive as TAKING THE BUS!

My job with a Fortune 500 company allowed me to do a lot of traveling by air. We lived in Atlanta. My sales territory was the Carolinas and both Virginias. Getting in and out of some of the towns there wasn't easy with commercial flights.

One evening in 1972, I had a 6-hour wait for a flight out of Roanoke to the small town of Lewisburg, West Virginia. The number of commercial flights was limited. But a guy at the bar told me about a charter service he used to get around the area. The charter service was over the border in West Virginia. Just for the heck of it, I called and asked how much they'd charge to come get me and to take me to Lewisburg. They said $60. That was less than the commercial fare. And, they said they could be over to get me in 40 minutes. I said, that's a deal and decided to do it. Canceling the commercial flight I had booked. Was easy in those days. The airlines were flexible with changes and cancellations. Trying to get an airline to make a last minute change today is tougher than finding a sympathetic parole board for Charles Manson.

Within an hour, my charter plane landed and pulled up to the terminal. I immediately figured out why it was only $60. The plane was an old 1940's vintage tail dragger. It had seen a lot of use, judging by the oil smudges on the engine housings. The pilot opened the door, got out and sauntered into the terminal. His battered cap was pushed back on his head. His jacket was open exposing a yellowed white shirt. His hands were in his pockets. I walked over to him, carrying my fashionably thin briefcase and suitcase.

"You Mr. Friel?" he asked in a booming voice. I nodded yes.

"Great," he said, with a big smile. "Nice evening to fly. Come on up in the cockpit with me. You can ride in the co-pilot's seat."

Heck, this was pretty cool. My own private airplane and pilot, and I get to ride up front. Why didn't I think of this before?

He quickly went through his checklist, and showed me where to plug in my headphones so I could listen in to the tower. When I was a kid, I'd wanted to be a pilot, so this was going to be an experience.

We took off. First time I'd ever experienced taking off up front and being able to see directly out the front of the plane. As we climbed out over the hills surrounding the Roanoke airport, he pushed his headphones off, and began asking questions about what I did, about my family, my job. He rambled about the scenery below, about his career. The guy was a marathon talker. I was his new best friend. He seemed to be paying attention to everything but his flying. He was turned facing me, left hand casually on the wheel, right arm draped over the back of my seat, as if he was kicked back in his living room.

We flew over remote mountains to Lewisburg, a small town nestled in the rolling hills of southern West Virginia. But we had to land in the neighboring town of White Sulphur Springs. I had heard the runway there was a little tricky. The approach was between two small mountains, and recently a small plane had crashed on the approach. All aboard had been killed. I was beginning to hope my pilot would pay a little more attention to his flying.

We started down. The plane went into a sharp bank to the right, so that I was looking almost straight down. My pilot kept up his discourse, talking now about the Model T Ford he was rebuilding. We leveled out and started down toward the hilltops. Ahead, I could clearly see the two mountain peaks, the narrow opening between them, and the runway in the distance. Captain Bob continued to talk, casually glancing out the windows from time to time. He hardly paid attention to the business of landing. He didn't seem concerned at all about the treetops coming closer and closer.

I was paying attention. Those trees seemed to be coming up pretty fast. And that gap between the mountains was narrow! The wingtips looked like they would brush the trees on both sides. I started to say something, but thought better of it. Hell, he was the pilot. He was a lot older than me, and obviously he hadn't killed himself yet.

We dropped through the gap. Miraculously, we didn't hit anything. I started to relax. Then I noticed we weren't lined up with the runway. We were going to miss it!

Captain Bob continued his relaxed banter, oblivious to the impending disaster. We were just moments away from a fiery, cart wheeling crash on the rutted muddy grass.

I couldn't keep it in anymore. I blurted out, "Captain Bob, we're going to miss the runway!"

He didn't bat an eye. In that same casual voice, he said, "Hell, boy; I never use the runway. Landing in the grass saves wear and tear on the tires."

I thought about immediately pulling out my Goodyear card and begging him to use the runway this one time, just for me. I would buy him a new set of tires that same day.

Captain Bob landed that old airplane as gently as he'd lower his granddaughter into her crib. We brushed over the grass at around a hundred miles and hour without so much as a bounce. And Captain Bob just kept up his running commentary.

Flying as much as I did back in the '70's, I got used to the occasional rough turbulence I encountered in storms at altitude. One day, I was flying from Toronto to Winnipeg. We took off under threat of thunderstorms. I was in an aisle seat near the front of the tourist section. My row mate in the window seat was a small, elderly gentleman who obviously didn't fly much. He was clearly nervous. His white knuckles gripped the armrest as we climbed through a light buffeting to altitude. About an hour into the flight, the buffeting picked up. We were into some rough air on the fringe of the thunderstorm, visible off to the right. Lightning flashed in the clouds in the distance. My row mate looked around nervously. I could hear his labored breathing.

Suddenly, there was a bright flash of lightning off the right side of the airplane. The sound system in the airplane ceiling began to buzz loudly. Even I was startled.

My row mate grabbed my arm and screamed, "What was that?" His nails dug into my arm.

I casually replied, "I think the plane just got struck by lightning."

He turned to me, his face drained of color. His lips quivered. "Then why don't the pilots tell us something?"

I probably should have taken his concerns a little more seriously, and said something comforting. Instead, I casually answered, "They're probably dead at the controls."

His eyes got wide. He began to whimper.

I immediately softened and told him that lightning strikes weren't uncommon, and rarely did any serious damage.

I doubt the old fellow ever flew again.

I have been through a couple of emergency landings over nearly 40 years of air travel, although nothing particularly serious. One time though, I thought I was on my final flight.

Several of us were on a morning flight from Toronto to Vancouver for a meeting. We were flying Air Canada, on a 727. It was a big plane with two engines on either side of the rear of the aircraft, and one tucked into the base of the tail. We were about an hour into what was normally a four flight. The stewardesses had just cleared the breakfast trays, and I had settled back in my aisle seat to read the Toronto Globe and Mail. Other passengers had reclined their seats to nap. The sun was streaming in through the small windows. The only sound was the white noise of the three jet engines. A smooth flight, well before the era of in flight phones, laptops, or air rage. Three more hours to Vancouver. Three hours to relax, read, or nap. Not a bad way to spend a morning.

Suddenly, there were three rapid-fire explosions in the rear of the plane. I jerked the newspaper in surprise, tearing it down the middle. I looked up and around to see what had happened. Other passengers were instantly alert.

Bang! Bang! Bang! Bang! Four more explosions. My mind went blank. I froze in my seat, expecting the plane to begin disintegrating. I had never experienced anything like this. This couldn't be happening to me. Air crashes only happened to other nameless, faceless people.

Bang! Bang! More explosions. Was the plane dropping? I looked around again. A stewardess struggled up the aisle, steadying herself on the seatbacks. Tears streamed down her face. Now I knew we were in trouble. Desperate trouble.

I looked forward. Passengers gripped their armrests and braced themselves, anticipating the break-up of the airplane in flight. But there was no screaming. No visible panic. Just quiet fear and dread on the faces I could see.

What was going on? Why didn't the pilots say something? I glanced out the window. The sun was shining. A bright and beautiful day 35,000 feet over Manitoba. And it occurred to me that this is how it would end. Within moments, there'd be another series of explosions and the rear section would began to tear away. There would be a roar as the plane decompressed. We'd be sucked out violently from our seats, into the collapsing ceiling and jagged metal of the dying airplane, to fall seven miles to our deaths. I hoped it would be quick, and that it wouldn't hurt too much. My thoughts turned to my wife, and children. At that moment, Agnes was probably in the kitchen doing dishes. Matt and Jennifer were in school. My mother was at home in Chillicothe, Ohio. I was struck by a black feeling, a deep sadness that I'd never see them again. Agnes would soon get a call from the airline, informing her of my death. She would go to school, and somehow break the news to Jennifer, 9, and Matthew, 7. How would they take the news? Agnes would call my Mother, and tell her that her son was dead in a plane crash in the wheat fields of Manitoba. All this flashed through my mind. The images were clear. The feeling of immense dark sadness deepened.

I will never forget the emptiness of that feeling, the dark helplessness of impending loss, .the absolute certainty that I'd never see my wife, my children, or my mother ever again.

And I am still struck by the absence, at that moment, of any panic or screaming. We all waited for the end. The seconds passed, turning to minutes.

There was a click overhead. The Captain keyed his mike. "Folks, we think things have settled down for now. We had some problem with our number three engine. We've shut it down, and the flight engineer tells me things look stable. So we'll continue on to Vancouver unless we have any more problems."

I could hear the sighs of relief, and nervous laughter as passengers began to loosen up. I turned to my row mate, who flashed me a strange grin. I suspected I had the same goofy look on my face. We were going to make it after all. Later, the pilot came back on the intercom. He told us that even though he didn't expect any more problems, emergency crews would meet our flight at the Vancouver airport. He told us how to assume the emergency landing position in our seats, to put the pillow in our laps, and face down in a braced position. Trying to further lighten the mood among the passengers, he said, "You'll have something to tell the folks at home."

We made our approach into Vancouver. The flight deck told us to assume our emergency positions. We neared the runway.

As we were about to touch down, I glanced out. There were the big yellow crash trucks below, lights flashing. My adrenaline instantly picked up. The 727 passed over the runway, and settled. A smooth landing. I could picture in my mind the crash trucks accelerating to full speed to catch up with us in case anything happened.

As the plane decelerated and began to roll to a stop, all the passengers began applauding. We were safe. We would walk away. After hundreds of thousands of miles in the air, it was the only serious incident I ever had. But the experience of being, at least in my mind, in a near death situation, is something I'll never forget. It was the beginning of my personal journey to understanding the meaning of the Three Priorities of Life and Business: Family is #1, God is #2, and Work is #3.

The company I worked for in Denver in the 80's had a private plane that we used for flying to our remote branches, or bringing customers into Denver for meetings. The plane was a turboprop King Air with room for eight passengers and a crew of two. We had a full time pilot named Drew. Tall and lanky, he was a perfect image of those legendary bush pilots who first flew the mountain routes. Marlboro Man good looking. Great mustache. Great sense of humor. Great pilot.

We always kidded our customers about taking an "insurance poop" before boarding our plane. It didn't have a bathroom; just a pee tube we had lovingly named "Sweet Lips". You went to the rear of the cabin, knelt down on your knees, and urinated (carefully!) into a funnel shaped device with rubber lips around it. Good thing most of our customers were men. We weren't sure how that design would work for women

We always had beer on the plane for those trips. So Sweet Lips got a workout, especially on long flights back to Denver in a headwind from points east. Sometimes, those headwinds were so strong, it appeared the traffic on the interstates far below was actually going faster than we were.

One day, one of our salesmen told a great story about bringing one of his customers to Denver from Grand Junction. Grand Junction was a six-hour drive west from Denver, through the mountains along I-70. Using the King Air, it was a forty-minute flight across the Rockies. It was a spectacular flight day or night. The scenery below was rugged, generally snow covered and forbidding, but incredibly beautiful.

According to that salesman, named Jim, he'd arranged for one of his customers, Butch, to fly to Denver to look at a piece of construction equipment. Butch was a housing contractor, and our company sold, among other things, the kind of front-end loaders Butch used in his business. Jim had driven over to Grand Junction, making calls along the way. He had arranged for our pilot, Drew, to meet him and his customers at the Grand Junction airport late in the afternoon. Drew would then fly Jim, Butch, and his partners to Denver for dinner and a machine demo the next day. Things began to unravel the afternoon of the trip. Drew had clearance problems getting out of Denver, so Jim and his customers repaired to the Junction airport bar to kill time. And to drink beer. A couple of orders of nachos later, along about 4:00 o'clock, Drew was still on the ground in Denver, so the boys ordered hot dogs. They thought by the time they got to Denver, checked into the hotel and drove to a restaurant, it might be as late as 8:00 o'clock, and the hot dogs would be just the ticket to tide them over. Besides, hot dogs go great with beer.

Finally, the King Air landed in Junction, and Drew helped the customers and Jim load their luggage. As usual, Drew had the big cooler full of Coors, Miller Lite, and Bud. After strapping in, they took off for the forty-minute ride to Denver.

As Jim tells the story, about fifteen minutes into the flight, Butch started to get a look of discomfort on his face and squirmed in his seat, as if to get more comfortable. He leaned over and whispered something to Jim.

Jim immediately unbuckled his belt, got up and eased forward to the cockpit.

"Drew," Jim said, "you got to land this plane. Now. Butch has to take a shit."

According to Jim, Drew looked at him incredulously. He gestured toward the windshield and the mountain peaks below. "Land? Where the fu*k do you expect me to land?"

Jim said, "Ol' Butch tells me he's never had to take a shit this bad. He's pretty uncomfortable."

Drew said, "Tell Butch it's 20 minutes back to Junction, or 20 minutes to Denver. See what he wants me to do."

Jim went back and consulted with Butch. Jim said Butch's face was red. His legs were crossed, and his eyes appeared to be bulging. After a hurried whispered conversation, Jim went back up front to talk to Drew.

"Butch says you have got to find a place to land. Right now. He's about to explode."

Jim said Drew raised his hands helplessly. " Jimmy, there ain't an airport between here and Denver. This airplane needs nearly a mile of straight, level pavement to land on. Look down carefully. Do you see ANYTHING that comes close to that? Tell Butch to hang on for 20 more minutes. I'll declare an emergency, but the tower's gonna ask what kind of emergency I got. When I tell 'em, they're gonna laugh their asses off."

Jim went back to Butch, and told him it'd be at least 20 minutes before they could land and get him to a bathroom.

At that, Jim said, Butch looked at him with disgust; grabbed Jim's briefcase, opened it, emptied out everything- all his papers, calculators, cigarettes, onto the floor. He eased out of his seat, wrestled his pants down, and shoved the empty briefcase under him.

Jim said it was a good thing it was one of those deep briefcases.

When they finally landed in Denver, Butch was the first person off. Didn't wait for Drew to open the door. He opened it himself, strode rapidly toward the terminal, threw the briefcase into a trash barrel and kept walking into the terminal without looking back.

I never asked Jim if he got the order for the loader.

Chapter 15

The Night I Blew My Chance at the C & W Hall of Fame

He was the star of a popular TV series during the 60's. Appeared in a number of movies. A tall, reasonably good-looking guy with a great sense of humor and comedic timing that Johnny Carson would have yearned for. His TV show went on for years, and his Las Vegas career continues to this day. His name is a household word. You'd know him immediately. You probably admire him, and may have seen him in person. He's still very active in show business. And, he's probably still very gay.

And he's the only human being who ever actively pursued me for a One Night Stand.

I must be the most naïve guy on the face of the planet. The day it happened, I was on a flight from Atlanta to Richmond. A "milk run," meaning a flight that stopped several times in route. This was probably late fall, 1972. One of the stops was in Greensboro, North Carolina. I was seated by the window, reading Newsweek. As the boarding process began, I looked up and noticed that the passengers coming aboard appeared to be entertainers. They were young, dressed in flower shirts and bell-bottoms, with long hair. Most had sunglasses in a variety of colors, ranging from very dark to rose colored.

The last person to board was Tim. I recognized him immediately. His hair was longer than he wore on his TV show.. And he was wearing a long mink coat. Not something he ever wore on TV, but it was definitely him. Tim Razor! Tim and I made eye contact, and I guess I must have smiled at the recognition of a big TV star.

"Damn," I thought. "That's Tim Razor!"

All the others went to the rear of the airplane. Tim took the seat directly behind me.

The door was shut and secured, and we taxied out to the runway. I was conscious that Tim was right behind me. A big star. One of My Old Man's favorite TV personalities!

Hell, I'm in a position to get an autograph for the Old Man. Or, for anyone else, for that matter. How should I approach this? What if I ask for an autograph, and he gets angry?

It didn't take long for my curiosity to be answered. I felt a tap on my shoulder. It was Tim, tapping me on the shoulder to get my attention.

"Pardon me," he said. "Do you know what that is down there?" He gestured out the window to the small town we were flying over.

I told him we'd just left Greensboro, and those were, without doubt, the Greensboro suburbs.

He responded, "Do you mind if I sit with you?"

I was flattered. Tim Razor actually wanted to sit next to me?

"Sure," I said. "Come on up."

He had taken off the mink, and was in a tasteful (at least, in the 70's) leisure suit. He took the aisle seat next to me. I don't remember all that we talked about, but he told me he was on tour through the South with his troupe- a few co-stars from his TV show, his band, and back-up singers. He told me he was appearing that night in Richmond, and asked if I'd like to be his guest at the show.

"You could watch the show from backstage. Come to the after show party, and later we could have a drink." This all came out very natural and easy. No suggestive overtures. Almost like one friend to another, making arrangements to get together.

I told Tim I was flattered, and that I was a big fan. Told him about the Old Man, and what a fan he was. Tim smiled at that, as if he was really pleased My Old Man liked him. But, I explained I was meeting my distributor Principal and some of his customers for dinner. A long arranged get together. I couldn't get out of it. Much as I'd love to see the show from backstage, and meet the band, I'd have to pass. The job had to come first. "Well, I wish you could be my guest," he said. "Where are you staying in Richmond?"

I told him I was staying at a Holiday Inn near the airport. Tim was booked into one of the fine old hotels in downtown Richmond. A suite probably. Rats. If I didn't have this stupid dinner to go to, I could rub elbows with a bunch of Hollywood types, drink champagne in a fine hotel suite with a Big Star. What a story to tell at the next sales meeting.

We landed in Richmond. The Distributor Principal was meeting my flight, and then we were going to work the territory. At least I'd get to introduce my associate to Tim.

Tim and I got off the plane together. Bill, my associate and the Principal of our Virginia distributor was there to meet me.

"Hi Bill. Shake hands with Tim Razor. He and I have gotten acquainted on the flight up from Greensboro."

Bill looked at me questionably, and shook hands with Tim. Hmmm….Bill doesn't seem to be as impressed as I thought he'd be. Tim shook hands with Bill, then turned to me, took my hand, and told me how much he'd enjoyed talking to me. Said he hoped we'd meet again. Then, he walked over to rejoin his troupe.

Bill looked at me. "What the hell are you doing with that guy?" he asked.

I told Bill the story of how Tim had boarded the plane, and asked to sit with me. I asked Bill, "What's the big deal? You're acting like he's an axe murderer."

Bill smiled, looked me in the eye, and said, "Don't you know that guy's a queer? Hell, everybody knows he's queer. Gay as hell! All he wants is what's in your pants!"

Bet Bill wouldn't have been so sarcastic if that was Tuesday Weld I'd introduced him to.

"Really?" I said. "You're joking! Tim Razor isn't gay…is he?"

Bill just shook his head. "Ed, you gotta start reading people better. Why else would some Hollywood star spend all that time talking to you?"

"Well, crap," I said to Bill. "I just assumed the guy spotted some latent potential for show business in my casual slouch in the window seat. Or maybe the Newman-ish way I wear my spectacles on the end of my nose."

Actually, my hobby at that point in my life was writing Country and Western songs. It had dawned on me that perhaps Tim might be the catalyst I needed to be discovered, and to get some of my songs published.

Bill and I left the airport and made calls on several of his customers for the remainder of the day. Bill was in his late 50's, a natural salesman and minor politician. He served on a committee of the Governor of Virginia. A very likeable guy, and fun to travel with.

That evening, we had dinner with Bill's partner. We were at a table in one of Richmond's better dining establishments. Bill was obviously known there, judging by the smiles and pats on the back from the manager, the bartender , and several waitresses. Bill told Norm, his partner, about my experience with Tim, and embellished the story out of all proportion.

Both Bill and Norm knew about my song-writing hobby. When you spend hours at a time in the car with a guy, you get to know a lot of things about him and vice versa. At one point, Norm grinned as he swirled the remains of his third martini, looked at me and said, "Hell Ed, this may be your big chance to get your songs published. And all it's gonna cost you is a blow job!"

Maybe I should'a kept the songwriting stuff to myself, I thought. Too late now. Hell, this story's gonna get legs and take off. But, still, the Old Man's gonna get a kick out of me actually meeting Tim when I tell him the story.

I just won't mention the part of Tim being gay.

Bill dropped me off at my hotel around 11:30 that night. Bill liked to drink, and we had spent several hours after dinner in the bar of the restaurant. Talking business, telling jokes, and second-guessing the management decisions of the Fortune 500 company we represented. This was still the early '70's, long before MADD, checkpoints, and the ban on open containers. Drinking in the business world is still around, but drastically toned down from those boozy days of the '70's. (The event described in Chapter 2 probably wouldn't happen in 2002). But, in 1972, relationships were built and solidified as much in bars as they are on golf courses today.

Come to think of it, things today really aren't that much different than 30 years ago. People in business STILL drink, and play golf. Guess the difference is, we just don't drink as much. Or we use designated drivers. Or take taxis!

It had been a long day, that day back in 1972, and I was beat. My flight to Atlanta left around 8:00 AM. That meant getting up by 5:30 or so to check in. I phoned the desk and asked for a wakeup call.

It seemed I'd just gotten to sleep in that Holiday Inn when the phone rang.

I came to, still groggy. Good Lord, I thought, it can't possibly be 5:30. I opened my eyes and looked at the digital clock. The red numerals came into focus, and my alcohol deadened brain slowly registered the time.

1:30 AM.

I picked up the handset. "Hello," I said, trying my best to sound bright and alert. In case it was my Boss. Or my wife.

"Ed," the voice on the phone said. "It's Tim."

My mind went blank. It was 1:30 in the morning. I was in a strange bed in a hotel- in where? Richmond.

My head hurts, and I'm talking to someone named Tim. I shook my head, trying to clear the cobwebs.

Before I could answer, the voice said, "It's Tim, Ed. You know, we met on the airplane this morning. I was just calling to see if you could come down to my hotel and meet me for a drink."

Tim. Suddenly, I was awake.

Tim Razor? He's calling me here? How did he track me down? What the heck does he want with me? This is a BIG STAR, and he's calling me? Am I dreaming? What do I say? Hell, I got Tim Razor on the telephone. He wants me to come down to have a drink with him? He's asking for me to come down to his hotel for a drink?

"Tim, wow. How did you know how to find me?"

Hell, the REAL question was, WHY are you calling ME? But, I didn't ask that. Maybe there was hope for C & W stardom after all.

"Hey Ed, you told me where you were staying. I just finished my show. Why don't you get a cab and come down to my hotel? We'll have a drink and get better acquainted."

This was like an out of body experience. I pictured myself, sitting on the Holiday Inn bed in my underwear, hair a mess, bloodshot eyes, talking to a big time TV and Movie star, with a string of record hits.

And he wants me to come to his hotel. For a drink.

Visions of Bill and Norm, smiling knowingly, swirled through my gin befogged brain.

How do I get out of this gracefully...without offending my ONLY contact who's actually a personality??

"Gosh, Tim," I stammered. "What an opportunity! I'd love to come down to your hotel. I've always admired your work. My Old Man is one of your biggest fans! But, sadly, I have an early morning flight to Atlanta. It's almost 2:00 AM. I'm beat, and I gotta be at the airport reasonably alert in just a few hours. Damn the luck!"

"Well, hey, Ed, I have to go to Atlanta tomorrow myself. What flight are you on?"

I reached over to my fashionably thin briefcase to find my ticket, conscious that I had one of the biggest names in entertainment in the world on the phone.

I was in my day old underwear, I was hung-over. Anxious to be LIKED. Anxious to be INTERESTING. So that maybe I could get him to listen to some of my stuff, to launch me into song-writing fame. And perhaps the C & W Hall of Fame.

Finally I found my ticket.

"Tim, I'm on the 8:40AM American flight to Atlanta."

Tim said, "Well, I have to go to Atlanta tomorrow too. Are you sure you can't come down tonight? I'd like to have you as my guest at the after show party."

I told Tim about my long day. Stressful meetings. Late night dinners. Entertainment with customers. And reminded him I needed to be up and alert in just a few hours. Much as I wanted to get to know him better, and somehow try out my songs on him, Norm's comment about the "price to be paid" painted a disgusting visual in the theater of my mind.

"Well, I sure wish you would change your mind," Tim said. He even sounded wistful. Visions of Johnny Cash singing one of my songs flashed through my mind, and I briefly wondered what a cab downtown would cost. Then thought about the smile on Norm's face when he mentioned the B word.

I said, "Tim, thanks for calling me and I hope we meet again."

"Maybe we will, Ed."

Man oh man! That unmistakable voice on the phone, and he's talking to me.

"Maybe we will. Good night, my new friend."

The phone went dead. I hung up, and flopped back onto the pillow. Had I just blown a chance to be famous? Had I just kissed off my ticket to stardom and riches? Crap, now I'm wide awake. I'll never get to sleep.

A major star like Tim had called me. Invited me to his hotel. I had needed a contact in show business if I was going to get exposure for my songs, and I blew him off.

Well, not really.

If I had been brazen enough to do that, who knows where it might have lead.

I must have dozed off, or passed out. Next thing I remember, the phone rang, and this time it was the operator.

"Five thirty, Mr. Free-all (man, that Virginia accent!). This be your wake-up call. You all get awake now!"

How the devil can anybody be THAT cheerful at 5:30 in the morning?

I got packed and caught a cab to the airport. Headed back to Atlanta and the office. The flight had already started to board by the time I got to the gate. (This was 1972, before security tightened up.) I looked at my ticket. 21D, well back in steerage. At least I had an aisle seat.

I entered the doorway of the plane. Turned to walk down the aisle, when a familiar voice said, "Hey, Ed!"

I looked up, right into the eyes of Tim Razor. He smiled widely, that familiar smile I'd seen so many times on TV.

"Hi Tim," I said, noticing that other passengers were looking at me curiously, probably trying to figure out if I was Somebody.

"See you in Atlanta," Tim said, as I went past, through the curtains and back to the cheap seats.

As I was buckling my seat belt, I looked up toward the front of the plane. Tim had turned around and was waving to me. Several passengers turned to look at me.

I could hear whispered conversation from behind me. "That's Tim Razor up in first class. Wonder who this guy is?"

The door closed and we pushed back from the gate. Tim was signing autographs, apparently. People in first class were handing scraps of paper and ticket envelopes to him.

About twenty minutes into the flight, the stewardess from first class came back to my seat. She handed me a note.

She smiled at me and said, "Tim Razor asked me to bring this to you." I looked up. Tim was looking back and waved. I waved back and opened the note.

When we get to Atlanta, stay on the plane. We'll get off together.

I looked up at Tim again, who was still turned, looking at me. He smiled and nodded his head, apparently affirming the invitation. I nodded my agreement.

The guy beside me nudged me. "He a friend of yours? Razor?"

"Not really," I said. "I just bumped into him yesterday."

My seatmate nodded, a smile playing on his face. What the devil was he thinking? Crap. I know exactly what he's thinking. I thought I could feel my face redden.

We landed in Atlanta. Even 25 years ago, Atlanta was a pain in the butt, airport-wise. Seems no matter where you were headed, you had to change planes in Atlanta. The standing joke was, when you die, and you go to Hell, you'll still have to change planes in Atlanta. Traffic around the airport was impossible.

I stayed on the plane as the other passengers got up and left. " Have fun with your friend," my seatmate grinned, as he got out of his seat. He looked at me and winked.

Hey, asshole, I thought to myself, if you were an amateur songwriter, you'd be looking for a break too. Everyone else had exited, I picked up my fashionably thin briefcase and started forward. Tim was standing in the aisle of first class, signing autographs for the pilots. He handed the scraps of paper back to them, thanked them for a good flight, then turned to me. "Hey, Ed, they've sent a limousine for me. Ride with me and we'll go to the First Class Lounge."

This was starting to get interesting. And complicated. I was in Atlanta. Home. Due at the office at some point. Wife and kids expecting me after work. What am I getting myself into? Still, this was turning into an adventure.

At the very least, something to tell the folks at the office. And at most, maybe a shot at having my songs listened to.

I got into the limo with Tim. The driver, a young black man said, "Welcome to Atlanta, Mr. Razor. I'm a big fan. Would you sign my trip sheet? My wife will flip when she hears I drove the famous Tim Razor."

Tim reached forward and took the clipboard, and asked for the name of the driver's wife. Then he wrote a brief note to her, and scrawled his name. I admit I was impressed. Tim was a gentleman. Humble. He actually seemed pleased at the recognition.

Tim turned to me. "Ed, I like you. I could sense the chemistry between us when we met yesterday. I have to go to Ft. Lauderdale to do a show tonight. Would you go with me? You'd be my guest. I'll pay your expenses. You could see my show from backstage, and then we could spend some time together afterwards."

So there it was. I looked at Tim. There was just a look of sincerity on his face. No leering. No sexual innuendo. Just a look of expectation. Hell, I was ready to believe he just wanted my company because I was such a friendly guy.

"Gosh, Tim. I don't know what to say. I work here in Atlanta, and I really need to get to the office." The limo was pulling up in front of the terminal.

"Let's go up to the lounge," Tim said. "We can talk better up there."

The driver opened our doors, and got our luggage out of the trunk. My fashionably thin imitation leather briefcase, and Tim's obviously expensive real-leather bag. The driver thanked Tim for the autograph, and shook my hand, studying my face to see which TV star I was. He had a quizzical look on his face as he studied me.

I followed Tim through the door and up the stairs to the first class lounge. The hostess recognized Tim, and asked for an autograph. She looked at me with a smile. Guess she figured I was somewhat out of place.

I was in a business suit, tie, and shoes that tie up the front. Tim was in expensive casual clothes. Dark slacks. A turtle neck. Patent leather loafers, and a soft leather jacket that probably cost as much as my car.

We sat down on a couch in a corner of the lounge. Tim ordered an orange juice. I think I ordered coffee. Several people in the lounge recognized Tim and came up to him to ask for an autograph. He was polite to everyone, and personalized each request.

After the last person left, he turned to me. "Ed, I hope your answer is yes. I really hope you can go with me to Ft. Lauderdale."

Visions of me in the C & W Hall of Fame floated through my mind. Then, a vision of me at 2:00AM tomorrow morning. After the after-show party in Ft. Lauderdale. When good ol' Tim might expect it to be SHOWTIME. And, exactly what would I tell my wife Agnes about why I was going to Ft. Lauderdale? I was pretty sure she wouldn't approve of me agreeing to a one night stand with the Pope, the Apostle Paul or, for that matter, The Virgin Mary, let alone Tim Razor. Not even if I was guaranteed a shot on Hee Haw.

The ball was squarely in my court. Time to fish or cut bait. "Tim," I said with some resignation. "As much as I'd like to go, I can't. I have a job here. And a wife and 2 kids. They're expecting me to be home tonight."

I watched Tim's face for anger or disappointment. There was neither. Instead, he seemed to smile and said, "Do you have pictures of your kids? Do you think the kids would like my autograph?"

I reached for my wallet and showed him pictures of Jennifer and Matthew. I don't remember what he said, but he signed the back of my ticket envelope with both their names. And added a note saying how much he enjoyed meeting their Dad.

Tim's flight was called. "Walk down to the gate with me, Ed," he said.

We collected our bags and walked out, turning down the corridor to his gate. When we got to the gate, Tim set his bag down, turned to me and reached out his hand. He took my hand in his, looked at me and said, "Are you sure you can't come with me?"

I smiled and said, "Tim, this is one of the most amazing things that's happened to me....but I have things I have to do."

He held my hand for what seemed like a minute....looked me in the eye. Still no innuendo. Just sincerity and friendship. Then he squeezed my hand, smiled at me and said, "Take care, Ed. Maybe we'll meet again someday." He released his grip on my hand, turned to board his flight, and was gone.

Tim still performs, and is just as popular as ever. I've been to events where Tim has been featured., But I've never made my presence known to him. Never tried to get his attention. Nothing ever came of my song writing. In fact, I haven't written a song in years. Not since The Night Ol' Willy Sang the Same Damn Song for Three Hours.

Chapter 16

My Old Man

My old man; Federal Prison camp; Mill Point, West Virginia

David Gates and his group Bread recorded a hit song in 1974 called, "Just to Have You Back Again". One of the lines, repeated several times is, "I would give everything I own….just to have you back again….just to touch you once again." A casual listener would probably assume this is one more love song about a boy/girl relationship gone bad. In reality, Gates wrote the song about his father, who had passed away the previous year; at least so I've heard.

I've identified with that song ever since learning about its origin. That's exactly how I feel about my Dad.

Funny thing, I didn't fully appreciate my Dad when he was living. I guess like any boy /man, I always wanted his approval. But I'm sure I must have disappointed him more times than I made him proud.

Dad was an officer in the Federal Prison System for 23 years. Started out at the maximum-security penitentiary in Atlanta. Then a transfer to a Federal Prison Camp in West Virginia, not far from his home which was across the state line in Virginia. I was born in the little hospital in Marlinton, the nearest town to the Camp itself, which was situated atop Kennison Mountain in the middle of the Monongahela Forest. The prison camp served as a supplier of forest products for the federal government; lumber for desks, buildings, and the like. There were around 300 inmates at that minimum-security facility, and probably a staff of 35 officers and civilian clerks.

Nine of the officers had apartments on the Prison Camp reservation, on a hill just above the long white dormitories that housed the inmates. Dad was one of those officers. There were no walls or chain link fences between the inmates and us, just a single chain, mounted on posts about waist high that surrounded the dormitories and mess kitchen. Signs on each post warned the inmates to stay inside the perimeter created by the chain.

Stepping over the chain was considered an escape attempt, and that carried an automatic 5 years added to the original sentence, plus a trip to Leavenworth. An escape attempt got the perpetrator hard time in a Maximum Security pen. But, most of the inmates at the prison camp were young first time federal offenders, or older prisoners no longer regarded as a real threat, so generally the days passed without incident.

One night, my parents talking in the living room awakened me. I was probably six years old. My brother, who could sleep through anything, was four. I got up and wandered out into the living room of the apartment. Dad was in his gray uniform, but tonight his pant legs were stuffed into combat boots, and he was wearing a gun belt. My little boy eyes were instantly drawn to the .38 caliber revolver in the holster, to the bullets in the loops on the belt and the handcuffs in a leather pouch. Dad had a rifle in his hand. He looked at me and said, "Eddie, better get back to bed." Mom turned and took me back to my bedroom. I asked, "What's wrong, Mommy?"

"There's been an escape. Several inmates are missing, and your Daddy has to go help find them," she said as she tucked me back into bed.

Wow, I thought, my Dad, with a real gun. Just like Gene Autry. Going out in the dark to capture escaped prisoners. I couldn't wait to get to school the next day and tell all the kids about my Dad.

Escape attempts were rare, but they did happen. A couple of the inmates would get homesick, or whatever, and simply step across the chain and disappear into the woods. Problem was, most of the inmates were from the city, or from other parts of the country, and didn't know those woods. This was a pretty remote place. Black bear country. Easy for a newcomer to get lost, quickly. It was nine miles to the nearest town, and at least 3 miles to the closest farm through the woods. The camp was situated in the middle of a thick hardwood forest, atop a mountain in one of the most remote parts of the state. Steep rocky hollows cut into the mountain. A swamp, known as the Cranberry Glades, bordered about 25% of the camp. It was a mosquito infested, snaky place, and a bad place to get lost. There was one highway that ran past the camp, and it was posted with warnings about the Federal Prison and the danger of picking up hitchhikers.

The officers, on the other hand, were from the surrounding area, and knew the woods and how to survive in them. But they wouldn't actually try to search the woods for the missing men. Instead, they would simply take positions on the highway, or on one of the many log trails, and wait. Eventually, after 3 to 4 days, the cold, wet, mosquito bitten inmates would stumble onto one of the officers stationed at a post, practically begging to be taken back.

Seeing my Dad that night, uniformed and armed made an impression on me. My dad was different from the other kids Dads. He had a real he-man's job! Roy and Gene had nothing on my Dad.

Dad, and all the other officers, had to qualify with a variety of weapons every six months, from pistols to sub-machine guns, Dad really didn't like guns. He often said, "A gun will get you into more trouble than it'll ever get you out of." He hated to waste a day shooting up all that government ammunition. But he did it, and was a good shot. He gave me my own .22 single shot rifle and taught me how to shoot when I was 10 years old. Guess he knew I was fascinated with guns, and he wanted me to know how to handle them safely.

One evening, years later, after we had moved to Ohio, Dad and I were watching Highway Patrol, one of the early police shows on TV. It starred Broderick Crawford. He played a plainclothes Lieutenant of the California H. P who carried a little snub-nosed .38 , and in every episode found a reason to use it. In this particular episode, ol' Brod shot the gun out of the bad guy's hand at a distance of 50 yards. Dad just snorted, "Look at that! You can't hit the broad side of a barn with that dinky little barrel. There's no way he could do that in real life." Dad told me once, "I'd have a better chance of hitting the crook if I threw that pistol at him, rather than shooting at him!"

The Prison Camp was under the jurisdiction of the Department of Justice and, from time to time, visiting dignitaries from Washington would visit the camp. They would always want to go into the woods, to see the logging operations first hand. The inmates were assigned to work details as loggers, equipment mechanics, or sawmill hands. Dad was in charge of the sawmill, and he frequently went into the woods to mark the tress that the logging crews would cut and drag to the mill with heavy equipment. Dad knew those woods like the back of his hand. He loved the outdoors.

One day, Dad had the duty to escort a couple of visiting Congressmen on a tour of the Prison Camp. They specifically asked to be taken back into the woods to see the cutting operations. Both men wore suits. Dad drove them in a truck up one of the logging roads to where the crews were working. It was in the spring or early summer. Dad and the Congressmen got out of the truck and started walking up the log road. One of the Congressmen said to Dad, " Mr. Friel, do you ever see any rattlesnakes in these woods?"

Now, Dad had worked in the woods for probably seven years by this time, and in all that time he had never seen a rattlesnake; but at that very moment, he spotted one just off the road. "Oh yes, Mr. Congressman; we see 'em occasionally. Why, there's one right over there!"

Dad said those guys couldn't wait to get back in the truck to get out of there.

I can still see my Dad the evening he came into the apartment after work, and announced as soon as he opened the door, "Well, I'm being transferred. Got my choice; Chillicothe, Ohio (a medium security Federal Pen) or Alcatraz."

That evening after supper, while my brother and I were in the living room, Mom and Dad were talking at the table over coffee, discussing the transfer. I remember Dad saying, "Only trouble with Alcatraz is we'd have to live in quarters on the Island. The boys would have to go to school on the mainland, and I don't think I want them on that boat every day going across the bay to San Francisco." A boat? Going to school on a boat? Sounded better than the smelly old school bus we had to ride every day. Where was California, anyway?

Dad settled on Chillicothe. Looking back, I don't think he ever was serious about Alcatraz. Too far from home, and Dad loved the mountains of Virginia and West Virginia. Chillicothe was only 6 hours away. And I'll bet every Federal officer was offered Alcatraz at some point in his career. Probably pretty hard to find men who wanted to live and work in that environment.

Years later, I visited Alcatraz as a tourist and saw the Officers Quarters where we would have lived. It would have been a real adventure to have lived on that island.

Dad was thirty-six when I was born. He'd had a pretty tough life as a kid. His own father died when he was young, and Dad had to work to help his Mom raise his six brothers and sisters. He finished high school, though, and later landed a pretty good job as a Regional Manager for Armour and Co. Even in the late 1920's, he had a company car and traveled a two state region, from his home in Richmond. I still have a picture of him as a young man, standing in front of a 1920 something Ford Coupe. When the Depression hit and he lost that job, he found work for a time as a tree trimmer for Davie and Co. in St Louis. But, needing to be closer to his home and brothers and sisters, he took a job as groundskeeper at The Greenbrier, an old-time, dignified railroad resort in White Sulphur Springs, W.Va. Beautiful place, the playground of the Vanderbilts, Rockefellers, many Presidents and other dignitaries.

To save money, Dad took a room with another dirt-poor young man from West Virginia, an aspiring golfer named Sam Snead. They lived together for a time, sharing a car, and often double dating. Dad remembered loaning Snead $5.00 one time, and that he was never paid back.

Dad told me that Sam once said, "Carl, why don't you go with me to the course and play a round?"

Dad told me he had never hit a golf ball in his life, but he went anyway. He used one of Sam's clubs, and on the first shot, caught it just right. Straight down the middle, about 250 yards. Sam looked at him and said, "Carl, you're a natural. Let's see you do that again."

Dad teed up another ball, took a mighty swing and missed it completely. He told me those were the only two swings he ever took at a golf ball in his life.

After I got older and was married, I thought it would be fun to see if I could contact Snead and get him to write a letter to Dad. Dad had long since lost contact with him, but enjoyed telling the story of Sam being his roommate at family gatherings. So I wrote to Sam Snead; told him who I was and my purpose in writing. About what a wonderful surprise it would be for my Dad to hear from him after all those years.

That was probably 1972 when I wrote my letter. Dad died in 1973. We never heard from Sam.

Growing up in those times toughened Dad. And working in the prison system produced its share of stress. My memory of Dad is of a quiet, somewhat stern man, as tough as a bar of iron. Just under six feet, black hair swept back (his early pictures resemble Tyrone Power), with a solid build. Devoted to his family, but certainly not a Ward Cleaver or Ozzie Nelson.

At Chillicothe, dad was assigned to one of the Prison industries. His detail had about thirty inmates. Chillicothe was a medium security penitentiary; most of the inmates were young, 18 to 35 years of age, serving time for Federal offences like car or mail theft; kidnapping, and bank robbery. This was now the early '60's. The times, they were a'changing. The prison system was starting to employ a new breed of psychologists and social workers. Inmates were demanding and getting more privileges like longer hair. "All those clowns think they're Elvis" my Old Man would say. "They got more TVs, more free time…and discipline's a joke."

From time to time, I'd hear Dad talking to Mom in the living room after supper when I was doing homework.

" I sent some young punk to the Hole yesterday for fighting," I heard Dad say. "Today he was back. He met with a social worker and told her he was mistreated as a child. She called me into her office and told me I'd just have to understand these boys. It's not their fault they broke the law; it's society's fault. That kid came back to the detail with a big smile on his face. There's no way I can discipline those men anymore. The social workers are taking over the system."

Dad was furious, his voice would tremble with emotion as he told Mom story after story like that. I guess it was too much to expect that Dad would be as relaxed and happy go lucky as Ozzie Nelson. What did Ozzie do for a living, anyway?

Dad was always close to his brothers and sisters and their families. We'd visit the aunts, uncles, and cousins as often as possible. One weekend, Dad and Mom traveled from Chillicothe back to West Virginia to attend the wedding of my cousin Butch, the oldest son of one of Dad's sisters. This was probably 1966 or so. Butch had met a girl from Washington, D.C. while attending college, and they were getting married on a fine spring weekend in Marlinton. All of Dad's brothers, sisters, and assorted relatives attended.

Apparently this young lady was from a fairly well to do family in Washington. I've never really understood why they got married in that small town in West Virginia instead of in Washington, but they did. Butch's father was Principal of the high school in Marlinton, not that that makes any difference.

Anyway, as Dad told the story later, they all went to the wedding at the Church, and then everyone assembled back at the home of Butch's parents for the reception. After an hour or so, the newlyweds went upstairs to get ready to leave for the honeymoon. Dad and his brothers John and Dan were standing at the foot of the stairs, in their Sunday best, talking. Dan had just complimented the young bride, saying to Dad and John, "Well, Butch has sure married a fine young lady. She's so polite and personable."

At that very moment they heard the bride upstairs say to Butch, "You have to get me out of here. If I have to spend five more minutes with these ignorant hillbillies, I'm gonna scream!"

As Dad told the story, he smiled and said, almost to himself, "That kinda hurt my feelings"

I was probably sixteen the first time I was locked up in a Federal Prison cell. I'd gotten my drivers license earlier that year, and like a lot of guys, decided that I'd look a little like Elvis if I let my hair grow. Dad tolerated my long hair, complete with ducktails and sideburns, but barely. Periodically, he said, "Why don't you get a haircut? You look just like those convicts I'm around all day."

One Saturday, Dad got up from the breakfast table and said to me, "I've got to run up to the Penitentiary and check on something. You want to go along?"

"You mean actually go inside the gates and see the place?" I asked. He nodded yes.

Now this was pretty cool to me, to have a chance to go inside the gates of a huge Federal Penitentiary. Past the guard towers. Across "dead man's" land, that space between the two chain link fences that surrounded the prison. Rumor was, and Dad never denied it, that the tower guards could shoot to kill if they spotted an inmate between the fences. Dad himself had been a tower guard in Atlanta.

I remember an incident that made the Chillicothe newspaper a year or so earlier. An inmate was spotted going over the high chain link fence. The tower guards fired a number of shots from their high-powered rifles, but never hit him. He was captured just outside the fence. The newspaper had a field day with their "guards who couldn't shoot straight" story and opined that the townspeople were hardly safe from those vicious felons, if the guards were so ineffective with their rifles. The Warden was forced to respond with some intense training on the range.

Shortly afterwards, another inmate scaled the first fence, and this time the guards nailed him with several .30-.30 rounds. He was taken to the prison hospital in serious condition. The newspaper howled about the use of such excessive force on a young inmate, just because he was climbing the fence. Dad got a kick out of the hypocrisy.

That Saturday when I rode with Dad up to the Penitentiary, I paid close attention to its layout. It covered probably a hundred acres. With that double chain link fence, topped with vicious looking razor wire, surrounding a number of green-roofed, red brick buildings. Towers were strategically placed around the prison compound. An armed guard manned each tower. We parked the car and got out, and walked to the main tower by the front gate.

"How's the weather up there?" my Dad called up to the Tower guard. I thought my Old Man was pretty quick to come up with that quip on the spur of the moment. The guard passed down a clipboard on a chain, and Dad secured his I.D. to it. Satisfied after he hauled it back up, the guard motioned us through the gate that he opened electronically. Then we passed through the second gate and started down the long walk to the Administration Building.

We went through the lobby of the Administration building and turned right to the first set of locked doors. Showing his I.D, the doors opened, and Dad told the guard on duty that he was giving me a tour. I thought I saw that guard wink and smile slightly. The guard opened a second set of doors after assuring the first set was locked behind us. Now, we were in the cellblock where, Dad explained, new prisoners spent their first month, locked in a single man cell before being placed in the general population. I was wide-eyed to be in that cellblock, locked cells on either side of the aisle. The doors were solid steel, with a small barred window looking out into the aisle. I saw faces behind several of the windows, obviously checking out the "new man."

We continued down the aisle, the floors spotless, our footsteps echoing, and the smell a combination of cleaning solutions and sweat.

Dad stopped in front of a cell. He said, "How'd you like to see what one of these is like?" I was hoping he'd say that.

I really wanted to see the inside, to see if it looked like those jail cells in the movies. "Sure," I said.

Dad looked back in the direction of the cellblock guard and motioned, and the electronic lock released. Dad pulled the door open, and I stepped in.

I heard the door close and lock behind me.

I turned to the little window and saw Dad walking away.. I turned and looked over my new surroundings. The cell was maybe six feet wide and nine feet long. A lidless stainless steel toilet. A small stainless steel sink. A polished square of stainless steel bolted to the wall above it as a mirror. A square of concrete, over six feet long and about 3 feet wide, along one wall was the bed. A rolled up mattress waited for the next occupant. A narrow window, too narrow to require bars, looked out into the prison yard.

I didn't want to touch anything.

I went over to the door, and looked down the aisle. No sign of the Old Man. Was he checking on his work? How long was I going to be in here?

I checked out the yard. Just a few inmates were on the walks. I felt stark loneliness. The reality of being locked up .

Dad came back and opened the door. "How'd you like it?"

I don't remember how I answered, probably something like, "Boy, that's pretty interesting." But I never forgot the experience.

Dad didn't say anything else. Not a thing, and never brought up the experience again as long as he lived. But I got the message loud and clear. He didn't have to say a word. I knew if I ever got in trouble with the law, or locked up in jail, that I shouldn't bother calling him to bail me out . I would be on my own.

I never had to find out.

The phone call came about 4:00 pm on Labor Day, 1973.

My wife, two small kids and I were living in Roswell, just north of Atlanta. We had several friends over for a Labor Day cookout. We were about to put the chicken on the grill. Creedence Clearwater Revival was on the stereo. The beer was cold and life was good. I had just been handed a major promotion with my company, I was going to Toronto to be in charge of all sales activities in Canada, the Yukon, and the Northwest Territories.

My wife answered the ringing phone. "Oh no, John…when?"

I asked her what was going on, but she held up her hand as a signal for me to be quiet, and continued to listen. Then, she put her hand over the mouthpiece, looked at me, tears welling in her eyes and said, "It's your brother…. your Dad is dead."

I took the phone. "John, what's going on?" John gave me the news. Dad had gone for his afternoon walk. It had been a hot day in Chillicothe, and when he got home, he got a glass of ice tea and went to the basement. He complained of being over heated and a little short of breathe. John and his family were at Mom and Dad's home for their own Labor Day cookout.

Dad liked to go to the cool basement in the summer and watch his favorite TV shows during the heat of the day. It was cool in the basement. Mom and Dad didn't have air conditioning. John said Dad told him he was going downstairs to watch "The Beverly Hillbillies," to cool down and get his breath back. Mom got worried about Dad and went down to check on him. She thought he was asleep in his recliner. She tried to wake him, shook his arm, and got no response. She screamed. John and his wife, a registered respiratory specialist, got Dad out of his chair and loosened his clothing. John tried to administer mouth-to-mouth resuscitation. John told me much later that his efforts caused an apparently involuntary vomiting response, and he actually got Dad's vomit in his mouth.

They called the ambulance, but it was too late. Dad was gone. Later, the Doctors told us the heart attack was so massive that, "Even if he'd had the heart attack in the hospital, we couldn't have saved him."

I hung up the phone. I was numb. I looked outside. The sun was still shining. Creedence was still playing. And yet, in the space of one phone call, everything was different. My life had changed forever.

My wife alerted our guests, and they gathered around to offer their help. We had to get to Chillicothe. Fast. I knew Mom would be beside herself. One of the couples offered to take care of the kids for the night, and send them on a plane the next day. After our guests left, we made the airline reservations, and called the family.

I started upstairs to pack. As I walked into the bedroom, it hit me. My Dad was dead. I'd never talk to him again. Never see him again. I broke down and cried for the first time in years.

Around 3:00 the next morning, we arrived in Chillicothe. We pulled up in front of the house in the rental car. All the lights were on. John came out the door, and we shook hands. I'm not sure what we said to each other.

In the house, Mom was seated in her chair. I went to her, knelt down, and took her hands. Tears streaming from her eyes, she asked me, "How will we ever live without him?" My throat was too thick to answer.

Later, when there was nothing left to say, we crawled into bed to get a few hours sleep. I awoke first, just as the sun was coming up. For a second, I didn't know where we were. Then I remembered we were home, the comfortable small home I'd known since 6th grade. It took a few more seconds before I remembered why we were there. And the bitter tears started again.

The next few days were a blur. The kids arrived from Atlanta. Other relatives came in from Michigan. There were a myriad of details: the attorney, the will, the bank accounts. And there was the funeral.

After a Masonic service at the funeral home in Chillicothe, his body was driven to West Virginia. We followed in our cars. Dad was buried in the shadow of his beloved Cheat Mountain.

John and I picked out the casket. Dad loved working with wood. He was a skilled forester, and spent much of his life working with wood, from logging to finishing fine furniture. We decided on an oak casket, a deep rich brown. Dad would like that, we thought. I dreaded the next day. The visitation, the first time I would see Dad in his casket. I wasn't sure I could do it. I didn't want to break down and cry in front of everyone. I couldn't be weak in front of Mom, John and the others. I had to be the strong one.

I wasn't sure how Mom would react, either. Would she collapse? Could she make it through four hours of greeting friends and relatives, while her husband lay dead just a few feet away?

I went to where Mom was sitting in the living room, and tried to prepare her. "Mom, tomorrow is going to be the worst day of your life. We're going to see Dad in a casket, and it's going to be a shock to all of us. Just try to be prepared. We'll be there with you." But who, I wondered, was going to be there when I fell apart?

The next afternoon, I drove to the funeral home with Mom, Agnes and the kids. We had an hour to be with Dad privately.

It struck me that life in Chillicothe was going along as usual. People were going about their business. Kids, on their bikes, laughing. I was on my way to see my dead father.

In front of Ware's Funeral Home, on a shaded street near downtown, I helped Mom out of the car. We all started up the front steps. Mr. Ware greeted us at the door. I remember the smell of flowers as we entered and the soft funeral music in the background.

"He's in the room just to your left," Mr. Ware said. He took Mom's hand to offer his comfort. We turned into the room. I swallowed hard as I took Mom's arm. The casket was at the front of the room, surrounded by flowers. Candles had been placed at either end of the casket. A large floral display was arranged on the lower half. The lid was open. And I could just make out my Dad's profile. I looked away, my eyes brimming. I held Mom's left arm. John was on her right, our wives and small children behind us. We walked slowly up to the casket. Mom just shook her head, as if in disbelief, and cried quietly.

We were at the open casket. I still hadn't looked directly at my Dad. I knew if I did, I'd lose whatever composure I still had. But I heard Mom say, "He looks so peaceful…."

241

I lifted my eyes.

He did look peaceful, eyes closed and lips forming the slight hint of a smile, the same look I remembered from countless times I'd seen Dad snooze on the couch. But then a realization hit me. That was not my Dad. He was not in there.

The Dad I knew was full of life, and love of nature, an avid reader, and a wonderful grandfather. That part of Dad wasn't in that casket.

It was true. All those Bible stories were true. How else to explain what I was seeing? My Dad, my wonderful Dad, was somewhere else. I'd never been a very religious man. I went to church when I had to, but I had a lot of questions.

In that instant, Dad taught me the most important lesson of my life.